Get Started Shorthand Pitman 2000

Edited by Mac Bride

For UK order enquiries: please contact Bookpoint Ltd, 130 Milton Park, Abingdon, Oxon OX14 4SB. Telephone: +44 (0) 1235 827720. Fax: +44 (0) 1235 400454. Lines are open 09.00–17.00, Monday to Saturday, with a 24-hour message answering service. Details about our titles and how to order are available at www.teachyourself.com

Long renowned as the authoritative source for self-guided learning – with more than 50 million copies sold worldwide – the *Teach Yourself* series includes over 500 titles in the fields of languages, crafts, hobbies, business, computing and education.

British Library Cataloguing in Publication Data: a catalogue record for this title is available from the British Library.

First published in UK 1986 by Hodder Education, part of Hachette UK, 338 Euston Road, London NW1 3BH.

This edition published 2010.

The *Teach Yourself* name is a registered trade mark of Hodder Headline.

Typeset by MPS Limited, A Macmillan Company.

Printed and bound by CPI Group (UK) Ltd, Croydon, CR0 4YY

The publisher has used its best endeavours to ensure that the URLs for external websites referred to in this book are correct and active at the time of going to press. However, the publisher and the author have no responsibility for the websites and can make no guarantee that a site will remain live or that the content will remain relevant, decent or appropriate.

Hachette UK's policy is to use papers that are natural, renewable and recyclable products and made from wood grown in sustainable forests. The logging and manufacturing processes are expected to conform to the environmental regulations of the country of origin.

Impression number   14

Year   2021

Front cover: © Shutterstock.com

Back cover: © Jakub Semeniuk/iStockphoto.com, © Royalty-Free/Corbis, © agencyby/iStockphoto.com, © Andy Cook/iStockphoto.com, © Christopher Ewing/iStockphoto.com, © zebicho – Fotolia.com, © Geoffrey Holman/iStockphoto.com, © Photodisc/Getty Images, © James C. Pruitt/iStockphoto.com, © Mohamed Saber – Fotolia.com

Contents

Welcome to *Pitman 2000 Shorthand*

Shorthand has a long history. When writing began about five thousand years ago, people must have noticed that while they could speak rapidly and listen to and understand what people said equally rapidly, it was another matter when they had to write the words down. For example, in English today, the gap between speech and writing is great. We can speak and listen at 140 to 180 words a minute, but we can write at only 25 words a minute.

From early days, people have been trying to find quicker ways of writing. There was shorthand in Roman times, and we know that Cicero, the great orator, had a shorthand writer. In Shakespeare's time some attempts were made (not very successfully) to use shorthand in order to pirate Shakespeare's plays. In Charles II's reign, Samuel Pepys wrote his famous diary in Shelton shorthand – a very good system, though never capable of verbatim note-taking.

Only in the nineteenth century, with the more sophisticated and scientifically based system of Isaac Pitman, did shorthand become a method of writing capable of recording speech accurately at speeds of up to 250 words a minute and, equally important, of being perfectly transcribed.

As the need for communications increased with the industrial and commercial revolution, shorthand found (and still retains) a place in the office. But shorthand is not just for secretaries and PAS. It is a valuable skill for any person who has, in the course of earning a living, to use words and writing every day.

Pitman 2000 Shorthand was first introduced in the early 1970s, as an improved version of the original Pitman New Era. It is easier to learn and more consistent in its application of the rules. It still has a speed potential of at least 150 words a minute, and is at least equally easy to transcribe into a handwritten or typed form with complete accuracy.

This book sets out to present the whole Pitman 2000 Shorthand with all its rules explained, including its phrasing principles. The points are illustrated with shorthand examples and with sentence exercises for reading, copying and writing. The accompanying audio has dictation exercises, linked to those in the book.

The aim is to give you a full knowledge of the system and help you to become a confident and competent shorthand writer. Becoming a fast writer is another matter. Advice is given from time to time in the course of the book to those who wish to write shorthand fast – that is, at speeds of 100 words a minute or above.

Pitman 2000 Shorthand is not hard to learn. Almost anyone can do it. All it requires is regular daily application and effort. Half an hour's study six days a week is better than six hours' study in two three-hour sessions. As with all skills, regular repetitive practice is needed, and the more frequent and the closer together in time these practices are, the more efficient and effective the learning will be.

Shorthand still remains, along with keyboard skills, a livelihood-earning qualification. Those who are well trained and competent in these skills and who have a thorough mastery of visual English still get jobs – and, indeed, much better jobs than those who enter office life without them. Electronic technology is changing the job of the shorthand-trained secretary, but it is certainly not eliminating it.

In any case, anyone who masters the system will have acquired knowledge and skill that will remain firmly implanted, like the ability to ride a bicycle or to swim, and that knowledge and skill is sure to be of lifelong value.

Only got one minute?

The essence of Pitman Shorthand, whether New Era (the older version) or 2000, lies in the following:

1 It is a system of writing based on sound and not on spelling.

2 Each of the twenty-four consonants of the English language has a separate stroke to indicate it. There is no such correspondence in ordinary longhand.

3 The consonantal skeleton of a word makes up its 'outline'. For example, the word package has an outline that consists of P, K, and J.

4 The twenty vowels and diphthongs of the English language are represented when that is necessary, and more often it is not, by a system of dots and dashes or other small and rapidly executed marks.

5 A number of abbreviating devices are used to show the common collocations of English sounds as, for example, ST and -ING and CON.

6 The most frequently occurring words in the language – words like and, the, have and for, and so on – have their own specific one-stroke signs. These are sometimes arbitrary, but more often based on their vowel and consonant structure.

7 Phrasing forms an integral part of the system. That is to say, two, three, four or more words may often be written continuously without a lift of the pen. There are well-tried principles of phrasing that enable this to be done. Phrasing adds greatly to the speed potential and writing ease of the system and in average English material, about 20 to 25 per cent of the words are phrased.

10 Only got ten minutes?

1 For the most efficient learning of Pitman 2000 Shorthand, it is best to study for half an hour or an hour each day.

2 Learning to *read* shorthand well is a great aid to learning to *write* it well. Repetitive reading is need to become a fast and fluent reader. All the shorthand examples should be read over again, until they can be read with no hesitation.

3 Do not move on to new material until you are sure you have mastered the section or part-section that you are working on.

4 There are many places in the text where you are given advice about how to write shorthand. In general, though, the following points always apply:

   (a) Shorthand should be written lightly. This is the most important single point to observe.

   (b) While all strokes are written lightly, you will learn from the start that some are written a little more firmly, and the distinction has to be made between those that are very light and those that area little heavier.

   (c) All the strokes are of uniform size.

   (d) For practice writing, use a shorthand notebook of good quality, smooth-surfaced paper of traditional size ($8'' \times 5''$) and with 21 lines to a page.

   (e) Shorthand is best written with a pen that is very smooth and fluent, and flexible enough to make the distinctions between light and heavy easily, or a special shorthand pencil.

   (f) Space out the shorthand words and phrases evenly and adopt a size about the same as that given in the text. This means that you should get an average of 10 to 15 words on a $4''$ line. It is convenient to have a left-hand margin of $1''$.

5 The short forms are very important. They are quick ways of writing the most common words, and they have to be learned by heart. This is not a hard task as there are only 144 of them. The fact that the short forms occur so frequently helps in learning. But they do need to be learned.

6 Pitman Shorthand is written phonetically – it is not concerned with the spelling of words, only the sounds. For example, in a word like *lamb*, we write the B in longhand, but the word consists of only the three sounds L-A-M and this is what we write in shorthand. Similarly, the spelling of a word like *bough* bears little relationship to the sounds we hear, which are just two: B and the diphthong OW – and these are the two sounds that we write in shorthand.

7 (a) There are exercises throughout this book. They are an indispensable and vital part of 'teach yourself'. If you work on them in the way outlined below, you will rapidly build up a vocabulary of the most commonly occurring words, increase your understanding of the rules, acquire accuracy, facility and speed in writing shorthand.

(b) Most of the exercises are presented in shorthand; a few are in longhand. Those in longhand are intended as a self-testing device. You convert the longhand into shorthand, and then check your own shorthand against that given in the key. Any mistakes that you make will reveal your weaknesses, and so you can concentrate on these and thus consolidate your knowledge of the system.

(c) The shorthand exercises introduce nothing new, but are based wholly on the rules, the words, and the phrasing that the preceding text has presented.

The first thing to do is to read each of the sentences or paragraphs. If you get stuck at any point, try to puzzle out the outlines, but do not spend too much time doing this. Refer to the key at the back of the book. The important thing is first to ensure that you can, without further reference to the key, read every word of the exercise. Equally important is the repetitive work. Go on re-reading, if necessary three or four times, until you can read unhesitatingly at 100 words a minute or more.

When that point is reached, but not before, copy the shorthand from the book into your shorthand notebook, There are 21 lines on a page of a shorthand notebook. Copy only on lines 1, 4, 7, 10..., etc. In this way you will finish up with 7 lines of copied shorthand, each with two blank lines underneath. If you have written the shorthand in the way suggested, you will have about 100 words on a page.

Do not do this mindlessly, but say the words quietly to yourself as you write them in. In this way you create the bond between what is seen, heard and written simultaneously.

Now, re-copy the shorthand using the first of the blank lines – once again being sure to say the words as you write them – and when you reach the end of the page you will be able to calculate your copying speed.

If when you start on the second blank line you can get somebody to dictate the page to you from the key, that will be helpful. However, when you have filled up your blank lines you can still test your own writing ability, if you have a watch or clock with a seconds hand, by writing the page (or the exercise) into shorthand from the longhand of the key. In this way you can calculate your 'free' writing speed. For example, suppose you wrote 110 words in 67 seconds, then you wrote 110/67 words in one second, and therefore 110/67 × 60 words in a minute = 98 words a minute.

8 At the end of many of the sections are texts for you to write as shorthand. These are also available as dictations on the accompanying audio, with each given at two different speed settings. Use the slower setting when you have first worked through the section. Come back and use the faster version at the end of the next section, to consolidate your earlier learning.

1

Basic strokes

In this unit you will learn:
- **13 consonant strokes**
- **how to show vowels**
- **about circle S and SES**
- **about short forms**

Consonants

There are twenty-four consonant sounds in the English language. Here are thirteen of them.

The first six are all written downwards:

$$\searrow \quad \searrow \quad | \quad | \quad / \quad / \quad \downarrow$$

  P   B   T   D   CH J

The next five are all horizontals written from left to right. Three of these – M, N, NG (as in *bank* or *song*) – are shallow curves.

  K   G   M   N   NG

The next two are written upwards, at an angle. L is a full-bodied quarter circle; W is a line, beginning with a small round hook.

L   W

Note that:

1 *The first eight go in pairs: P-B, T-D, CH-J, K-G. Each pair has the same sound except that the more firmly written of the pair is voiced, and the very light one of the pair unvoiced. That is to say, the vocal cords are used for voiced consonants, but not for the unvoiced ones.*

2 *All the consonants are the same length.*

CONSONANTS JOINED

Two or more of these consonants can be written one after another without taking the pen from the paper, forming an *outline* for a word.

Writing notes

When two or more consonants are written together there should be no appreciable pause between ending one stroke and beginning the next. Write very lightly even when making the distinction between such stroke as T and D. Write the outline first, and insert the vowels afterwards.

EXERCISE 1

Practise writing the thirteen consonants several times, then practise the consonants joined to form outlines, as shown here.

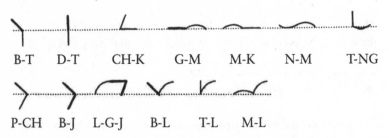

| B-T | D-T | CH-K | G-M | M-K | N-M | T-NG |

| P-CH | B-J | L-G-J | B-L | T-L | M-L |

Vowels

English has twenty vowels and diphthongs. In this section, we are dealing with eight vowels. Vowels are written with either dots or short dashes, and at set places on the lines – we will come back to the places in a moment.

Vowels	*How written*	*Examples*
AY as in gate	heavy dot	aim may gate
OH as in code	heavy dash	ode dough code
E as in bet	light dot	etch gem bet
U as in cub	light dash	up lung cub
AH as in palm	heavy dot	calm pa palm
AW as in bought	heavy dash	law awl bought
A as in pack	light dot	am map pack
O as in lock	light dash	odd job lock

The first four vowels are all second-place vowels. Any consonant has three places for vowels to be written, according to the direction in which the consonant stroke is written:

The first rule is simple: if the vowel comes before the consonant, it is written before it, and if it comes after the consonant, it is written after it. The examples will make this clear:

| up | pay | ale | low | oak | go |

Dash angles

Notice that dash vowels are at right angles to the stroke at the point where they are written.

Position of outlines

These two rules run all the way through shorthand:

1 *The first vowel in a word decides where the outline for that word will be written – above, on, or through the line.*
   ▷ *With first place vowels, the outlines go above the line*
   ▷ *With second place vowels, the outlines go on the line*
   ▷ *With third place vowels, the outlines go through the line.*
2 *Is it the first upward or downward stroke that goes above, on or through the line. If the outline consists only of horizontal strokes, they are written above, on or through the line.*

In the table of eight vowels shown above, the first four (AY, OH, E and U) are all second-place vowels. Their outlines all sit on the line.

The second group of four vowels (AH, AW, A and O) are first-place vowels. Therefore they were written above the line.

Here are the outlines for six more words illustrating these two rules:

page   load   gap   lodge   name   gong

EXERCISE 2

Read then copy the following words:

aim	know	own
beg	memo	mail/male
date	~~effect~~	cope
tape	top	lack
knock	bought	aid
day	much	locate
dock	chalk	bank
long	get	jet
age	edge	tell
tale	coal	pole
gaol/jail	catch	coach
back	beg	way
away	watch	well
wall	web	wade

Write the following words in shorthand then check against the key at the end of the book:

(a)	long	get	jet	age	edge	tell	tale
(b)	gate	pail	gaol/jail	catch	coach	back	beg
(c)	way	away	watch	well	wall	web	pack

Circle S

A small circle may be written at the beginning or at the end of any consonant. Initially it represents the sound of S, Finally it may represent the sound of S or Z. An initial S is read first. A final circle S is read last. That means that you cannot have a vowel before an initial circle S, and you cannot have a vowel after a final circle S.

Some examples of circle S in use:

aim	aims	same	some
maize	sad	soap	pose
oats	toes	aids	days
chose	ages	sage	snow
knows	song	sung	sunk
low	slow	sole	sales
smoke	spade	such	scales
stay	stays	set	sets
sense	memos	ways	suppose

SES circle

Nouns ending in the S or Z sound have plurals ending SES or ZEZ (pace, paces; phase, phases). Verbs ending in S or Z have a third person singular of the present tense which ends in SES or ZEZ (I guess, he guesses; you laze, she lazes). The sound also occurs in other words. It can be shown by writing a large final circle – called the SES circle.

Here are some examples:

pass	passes	base	bases
guess	guesses	chase	chases
loss	losses	pace	paces
case	cases	space	spaces
sense	senses	dose/doze	doses/dozes
excess	access/axes	box	boxes

The suffix -ING

-ING is a very common suffix to verbs. This is shown by a dot placed at the end of the consonant that precedes it. Dot -ING is used only for verbal suffixes: it is not used for words like *king, sting, awning, etc.*

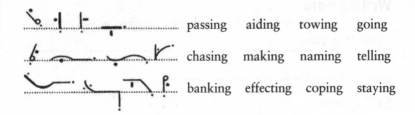

	passing	aiding	towing	going
	chasing	making	naming	telling
	banking	effecting	coping	staying

Practise writing the SES words and the -ING words.

SHORT FORMS

Very common and frequently occurring words are represented by shortened outlines and these all have to be learned by heart. Here are the first 29.

Copy and memorise them:

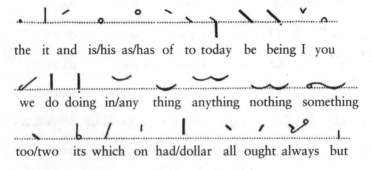

the it and is/his as/has of to today be being I you

we do doing in/any thing anything nothing something

too/two its which on had/dollar all ought always but

The direction in which short forms are written, and their position in relation to the line are important.

Some short forms are very short strokes for very common words, and these strokes are arbitrary, for example, *and, of, on* and *but*. The short form *and* is written upwards.

Most short forms, however, have consonant strokes and a position in relation to the line that relates to the missing vowels; for example *anything* and *nothing* have identical short forms but one sits above the line and the other on it.

Notice that *to* and *too/two* form a pair, light and heavy.

Write the circles for *is/his* and *as/has* round to the left – anticlockwise, ⤴......

Phrasing

It is often possible to write two or three or more words in shorthand as one continuous outline without a lift of the pen. There are principles of phrasing which will be explained as we proceed.

Phrasing increases the ease, speed and readability of shorthand, and it is therefore a craft to be cultivated. But it has its rules and these must be observed.

Circle S for us

The circle S may be used in phrases for *us*:

ͺo	ͽ	b
to us	of us	on us

These phrases should be practised.

Tick THE

Though there is a short form for *the*, the commonest word in the language, it is far more usual to make use of a tick as in these phrases:

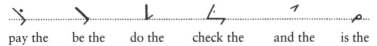

ͻ	ͻ	ι	ι	⌐	ρ
pay the	be the	do the	check the	and the	is the

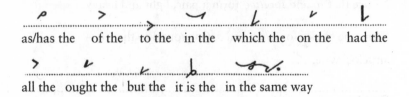

as/has the   of the   to the   in the   which the   on the   had the

all the   ought the   but the   it is the   in the same way

These phrases should be practised. Notice that the phrases *on-the* and *but-the* are given a slight slant to make them easier to write and read.

Which way?

Tick THE is always the same in appearance, but sometimes it is written upwards and sometimes downwards. The rule is simple: tick THE can only be written after a stroke, and is written in the direction that gives the sharper angle.

Punctuation

Punctuation is the same in shorthand as it is in longhand, except for:

full stop .....✗.... question mark .....✗.... exclamation mark .....✗....

dash .... hyphen .....⁓...... parentheses (brackets) .(.......).

To show a capital letter, two short light dashes ⁄ are written upwards below the outline, as in:

Tom .... Monday ....

EXERCISE 4

First read the sentences, without the key if possible. Then copy them, writing as quickly as you can while still concentrating on accurate, well-formed outlines like those in the text. Say the words to yourself as you write.

Follow these instructions for all other shorthand exercises in this and subsequent sections:

(a) 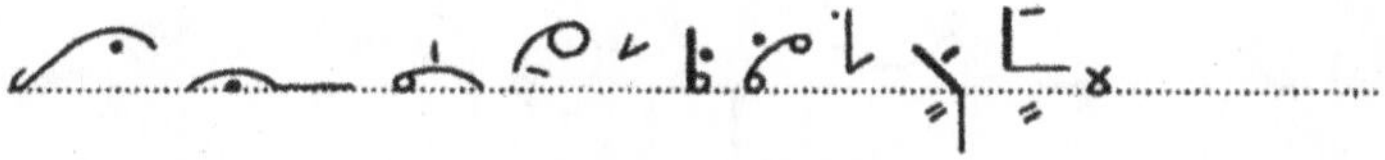 [shorthand outlines]

(b) 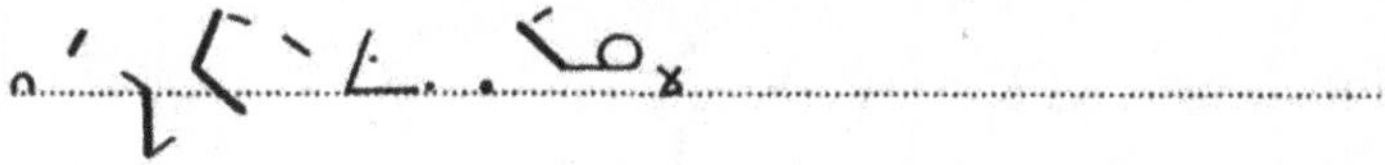 [shorthand outlines]

(c) 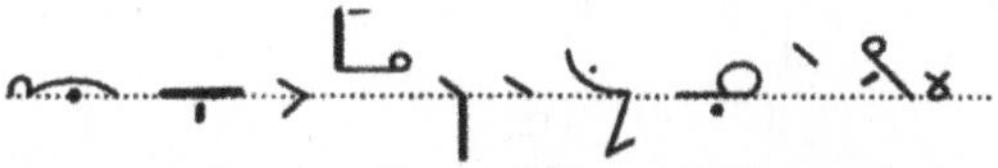 [shorthand outlines]

(d)  [shorthand outlines]

(e) 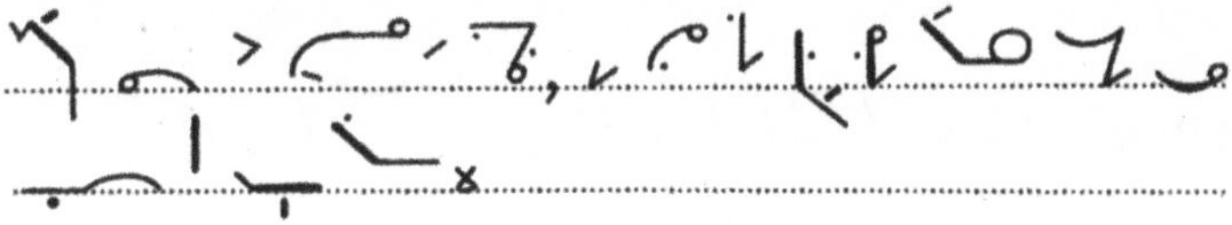 [shorthand outlines]

(f)  [shorthand outlines]

(g) 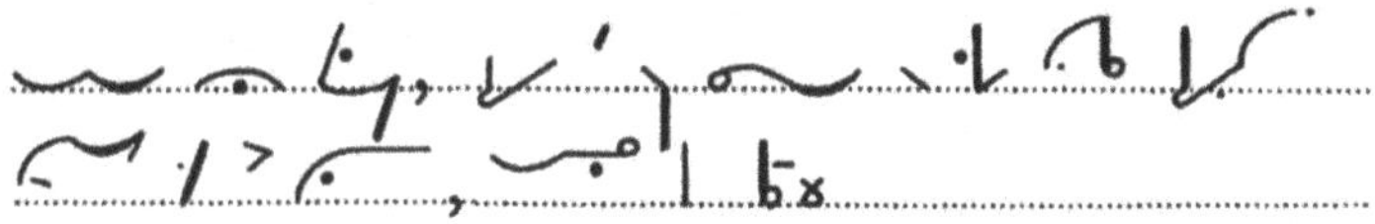 [shorthand outlines]

(h) 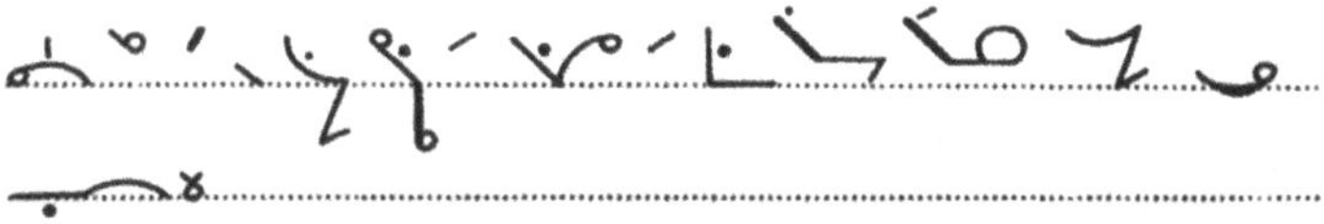 [shorthand outlines]

(i) 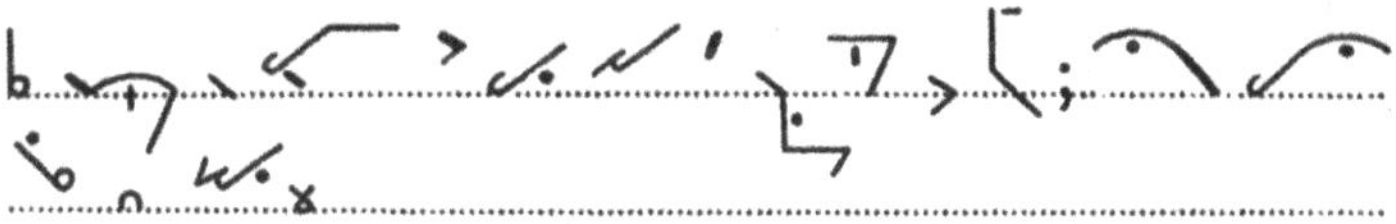 [shorthand outlines]

(j)

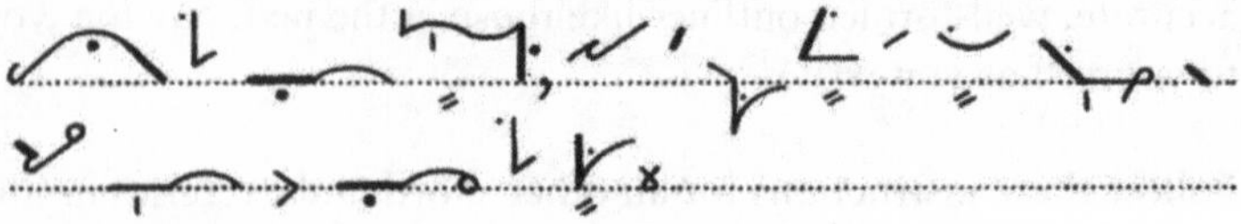

EXERCISE 5

(a)

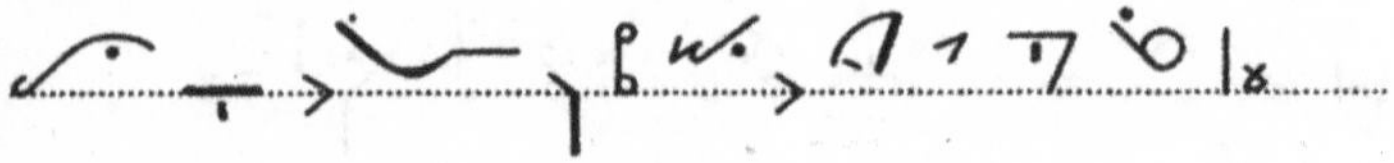

(b)

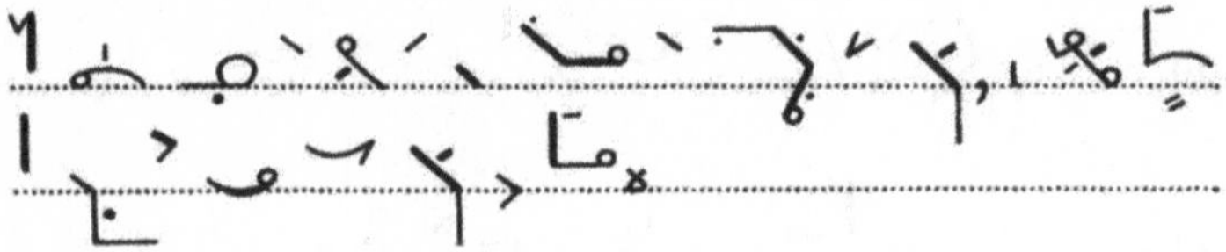

(c)

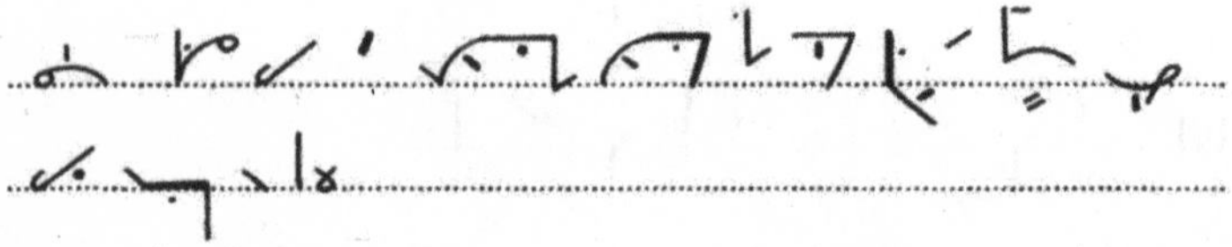

(d)

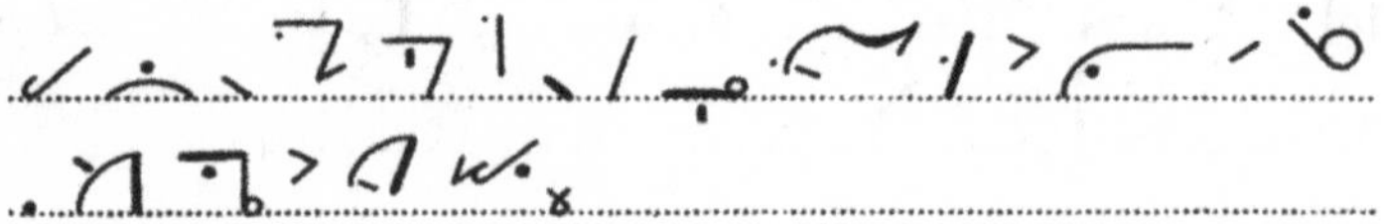

(e)

EXERCISE 6

Write the following in shorthand (phrasing is shown by the hyphens):

(a) We ought to-take two of-the boats up to-the lake today.

(b) I-know something you ought to-do; you ought to bank-the cheques today.

(c) It-was snowing along-the edge of-the bay and-I-had no mac.

(d) Take all-the baggage to-the docks and stow it in-the space which-the dock allocates to-us.

(e) We ought to know-the name of-the tape, because it-is-the same as-the tapes we bought at-the sale on-Monday.

Dictation time

This exercise is present in the form of dictations on the audio. Try Ex 6.A now before going on to Unit 2.

THINGS TO REMEMBER

▶ *Shorthand is based on how words sound, not how they are spelt.*

▶ *Consonants form the outline of the word.*

▶ *Vowels are marked by dots and dashes. Their position in relation to the consonants is important.*

▶ *The first vowel decides whether an outline sits above, on or through the line.*

▶ *There are short forms for the most common words and phrases.*

▶ *With verbs, a dot at the end of an outline adds -ING.*

▶ *You can show 'the' by writing a tick at the end of an outline.*

2

Consonants and vowels

In this unit you will learn:
• **seven more consonant strokes**
• **how to show the past tense**
• **about stress in words**
• **how to indicate vowels**

Seven more consonants

Here are a further seven consonants:

　F　　V　Th　TH　S　SH　Y

The first four of these are pairs, the light stroke being the unvoiced sound and the heavy stroke the voiced sound.

The difference between the Th/TH forms is that heard in the words *thick* (unvoiced) and *those* (voiced).

F, V and SH are full-bodied quarter circles. Th, TH and the stroke for S are shallow curves.

All are written downwards except for Y, which begins with the small round hook and goes upwards. Compare ......✓........ W and ......✓...... Y.

These outlines show the new consonants in use, along with the consonants and vowels given in Section 1. They should be read and copied:

				fame	photo	safe	save
				faith	facts	cafe	follow
				vote	love	vague	vale/veil
				face/phase	faces/phases	them	those
				though	path	maths	oath
				loth	loathe	thatch	yell
				yellow	Yale	yes	yolk
				show	showing	shape	shops
				cash	shed	shallow	shell
				wash	washing	they	chef

Stroke S

Stroke S is used in three situations:

1 *When S is the only consonant in the word:*

so   us   say   essay   saw

2 *When a vowel precedes an intial S or follows a final S:*

ask escape essences peso Nassau

This is one of the many devices in shorthand which enable us

to dispense with vowels. For example, 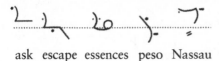 *........... must begin*

with S (and so is either sack *or* sock*), whereas*  *........... must*

begin with a vowel before the S (and must be ask*).*

3 *When a word begins with S + vowel + S/Z:*

sausage Sussex

HOW CIRCLE S IS WRITTEN WITHIN OUTLINES

We saw in Unit 1 that when S is the first sound in a word, or S/Z is the last sound in a word, then we write a circle S. That circle is written inside curves and anticlockwise. .... to straight strokes:

sex sense

S or Z in the middle of a word is also written with the small circle S. In such cases, which are very common, the S is written as follows:

Where straight strokes meet, the circle is written outside the angle, either clockwise or anticlockwise as needed:

desk task bestow cassette gazette custom

Inside curves, whether the curves are alone or before or after a straight stroke:

mass message mask chosen dozen tassel

Inside the **first** curve when two curves are separated by S/Z:

fasten unsafe mason lesson

Notice in the last two examples how the circle is completed before the next consonant is written.

There are special rules before S/Z and L. After downward curves F, V, Th, TH or after an N, the circle is only taken far enough for the following L to be written out of it:

vessel nestle nozzle senseless

Review the rules

Read through the circle S rules again, and copy out each example. The sense behind each rule becomes clear once you start to use them.

EXERCISE 7

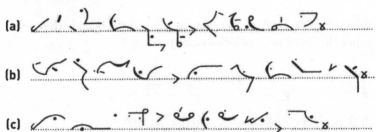

(a)

(b)

(c)

(d) [shorthand outline]

(e) [shorthand outline]

Past tense of regular verbs

Regular verbs are those that have only four forms like *touch*.
The forms are *touch, touches, touching, touched*. Most verbs are
regular.

The past tense of all regular verbs in English ends in the sound of
either T or D. To write such past tenses, *disjoin* the T or D stroke
and write it close up.

Disjoining

Disjoining – writing part of the word separately – is used in
certain situations to make an outline easier to read. We will
come back to this in Section 23.

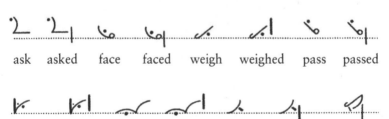

| ask | asked | face | faced | weigh | weighed | pass | passed |

| delay | delayed | mail | mailed | show | showed | washed |

| dated | loved | packed | locked | cashed | loaded |

The consonant R

When an R appears in the spelling of a word, it always appears
in the shorthand, even though it may not seem to be sounded.
The main reason for this is that always including the R makes
it much easier to read the outline. A second reason is that the
presence of an R often modifies the vowel that precedes it.

Because R is a very common consonant, there are two ways
of writing it. There is a straight stroke written upward
and a full-bodied curve written downwards . These are
both light strokes.

Upward R is written at an angle, so the following stroke joins
at the top, and this ensures that it can never be mistaken
for CH where the follow-on stroke is at the bottom.
Compare .... and ....

     CH-K   R-K

The rules for writing

1 *R is always written downward before M:*

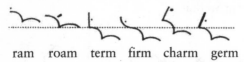

  ram   roam   term   firm   charm   germ

(Note how the ER vowel is written in term *and* firm.*)*

2 *R is written upwards when it is the first sound in a word:*

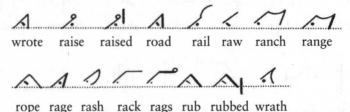

  wrote   raise   raised   road   rail   raw   ranch   range

  rope   rage   rash   rack   rags   rub   rubbed   wrath

3 *R is written upwards in the middle of an outline:*

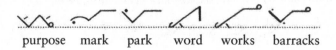

purpose   mark   park   word   works   barracks

4 *R is written upwards when it is the last consonant in a word and is followed by a vowel sound:*

burrow   borrowed   morrow   narrow   thorough   marrow

5 *R is written downwards when R is the first consonant in a word and is preceded by a vowel:*

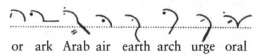

or   ark   Arab   air   earth   arch   urge   oral

6 *R is written downwards at the end of an outline when R ends the word:*

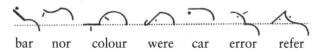

bar   nor   colour   were   car   error   refer

7 *The common words ending in the -ARE sound (however they are spelled) are written with the AY vowel, second-place heavy dot:*

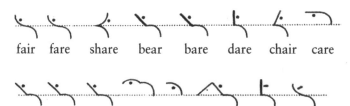

fair   fare   share   bear   bare   dare   chair   care

pair   pare   pear   mare   air   repair   door   four

8 *The common words ending in the -ORE sound are written with the OH vowel, second-place heavy dash, as in:*

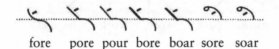

fore   pore   pour   bore   boar   sore   soar

9 *When downward R is used in a root outline, it is retained in any words derived from that root, as in:*

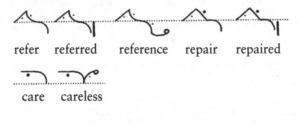

refer   referred   reference   repair   repaired

care   careless

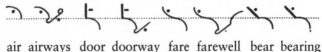

air airways door doorway fare farewell bear bearing

10 *Circle S or SES maybe added to final downward R:*

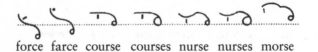

force farce course courses nurse nurses morse

INDICATING VOWELS AROUND R

Having studied how upward and downward R are used, you will see that we have a way of showing vowels without the need to write them in.

If we see a downward R as the first consonant in an outline, then (unless it precedes M) we know there must be a vowel before it. The position of the outline will give us the clue to the vowel. For example, in .... there must be a vowel before the R and the vowel must be first-place, so the word is *ark*.

Unstressed vowels

Many two-syllable words end in -AGE, unstressed, such as *cabbage* and *package*. The second-place light dot is used for such unstressed vowels.

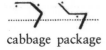

cabbage package

In words like *custom* and *colour*, the second vowel is unstressed and unclear in sound. The second-place light dash is normally used for such words.

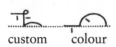

custom   colour

Many words have an ER vowel, and this is stressed in words like *purse* and *jerk*, but unstressed in words like *above* and *visa*.

purse   jerk

ER vowels are normally treated as follows:

1 *If it is spelled* i *or* y *as in fir or birth, or with* e *or* ea *as in earl or term, use the second-place light dot:*

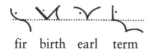

fir   birth   earl   term

2 *If it is spelled with* o *or* u *as in work or fur, use the second-place light dash:*

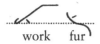

work   fur

Sometimes spelling does count

Though it's normally the sound of a word, not its spelling, that determines its outline, there are a few special situations where spelling does count. The ER sound is one of these. And why? Basically, because this is very common, and relying on sound alone could cause confusion. There's a good example here with *fir* and *fur*.

SHORT FORMS

Copy and memorise:

for	have	having	this	thank	thanks	thanking	thanked	a/an

with	will	willing	yesterday	are	hour/our	hours/ours

ourselves	your	yours	yourself	manufacture	manufactures

manufactured	manufacturers	manufacturing	that	think	thinks

thinking	owe	owes	owed	owing	although	tomorrow	shall

Notes on short forms

(a) with *is a small light anticlockwise semicircle written in the first position (above the line).*

(b) *The short forms for* will, willing, hour/our, hours/ours, ourselves *are all written through the line.*

(c) *Notice how many short forms like* thank *may have circle S, dot -ING and disjoined T or D added just like other regular verbs.*

(d) *The short form for* that *is a heavy TH above the line, but half the length of a normal TH.*

Consolidate

The best way to remember short forms is to keep practising them. Go back now and look again at the short forms in Section 1.

Phrasing
Practise:

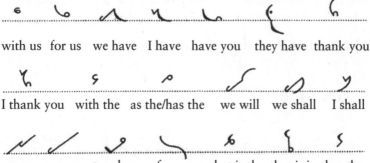

with us   for us   we have   I have   have you   they have   thank you

I thank you   with the   as the/has the   we will   we shall   I shall

are we   we are   two hours   for your   that is the   that it is   that the

I think   I think we are   we think you are   although we are   I shall be

NOTES ON PHRASES

In some phrases the short form you may be turned to give an easily written join:

and you   are you   with you   will you

In phrases *like I-thank-you* and *that-it-is* and *I-think*, the position of the phrase may be adjusted so that the second word of the phrase, as well as the first, is written in its correct position.

Intersections

One stroke may be struck through a preceding one to represent a commonly occurring word, as in:

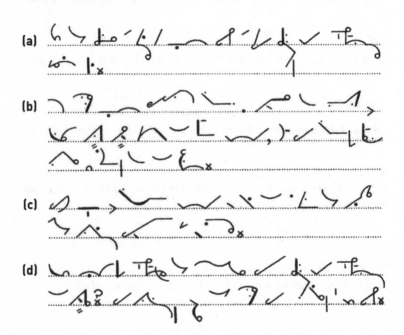

.... bank   .... bank charge

.... customs   .... customs form

There are thirteen of these intersections in Pitman 2000 Shorthand and *charge* and *form* are the first two of these. A circle S may be added for the plural or to show the possessive, as in:

.... your charges   .... despatch forms

EXERCISE 8

(a)

(b)

(c)

(d)

(e)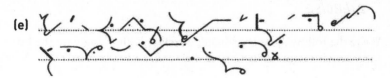

(f)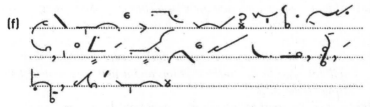

(g)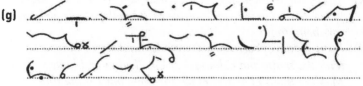

(h)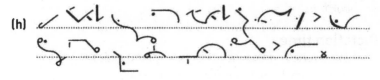

(i)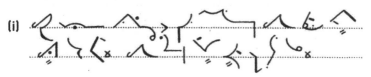

(j)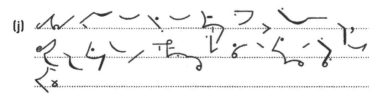

EXERCISE 9

Write the following in shorthand, afterwards checking with the key (phrasing is indicated by hyphens):

(a) *May-we ask-you to vote for-us on-Thursday? Supposing we-are elected, we-shall-do much to-get your rates and taxes paid.*

(b) *Some of-us will-have to pay-the dock-charges today or they-will take our boxes to-the customs and it-will take-us months to-get them back.*

(c) *They-have worked long hours for-us, and-I-think-we ought to ask them to-come with-us to-the Bungalow Cafe and pay for-them, too.*

(d) *I-saw a pair of vases in a shop today and so fell in love with-the shape and colours that I walked in and bought them. Maybe I-had to pay too-much for-them but I-think they-are worth it.*

Dictation time

This exercise is present as dictations on the audio. Try Ex 9.A now, then try Ex 6.B before going on to Unit 3.

THINGS TO REMEMBER

▶ *S is written with a stroke to allow vowels to be shown.*

▶ *A disjoined D stroke adds -ED to make verbs past tense.*

▶ *R can be written with a straight up stroke, or a curved down stroke.*

▶ *Unstressed vowels are shown by a second place light dot or dash.*

3

Halving strokes

Halving to add T

In words of only one syllable, any light stroke may be halved to add the sound of T. Circle S may be added to the half-length stroke.

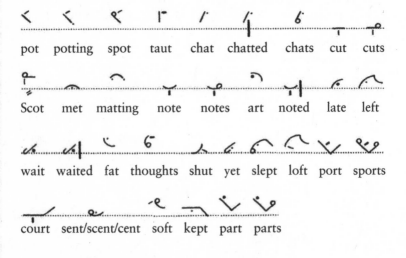

| pot | potting | spot | taut | chat | chatted | chats | cut | cuts |

| Scot | met | matting | note | notes | art | noted | late | left |

| wait | waited | fat | thoughts | shut | yet | slept | loft | port | sports |

| court | sent/scent/cent | soft | kept | part | parts |

Halving to add D

In words of only one syllable, a heavy stroke may be halved to add the sound of D, but note that the heavy stroke NG is not halved. Circle S may be added to the half-length stroke.

bed beds bedding bad dead goad goaded

EXERCISE 10

(a)

(b)

(c)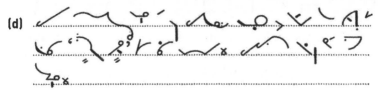

(d)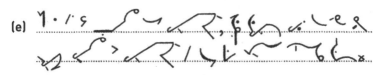

(e)

HALVING IN WORDS OF MORE THAN ONE SYLLABLE

In words of more than one syllable, a stroke may be halved to
show either a following T or D.

expect   expects   method   except   result   remote   deduct

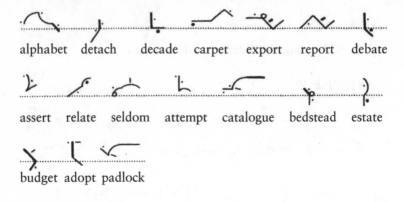

alphabet   detach   decade   carpet   export   report   debate

assert   relate   seldom   attempt   catalogue   bedstead   estate

budget adopt padlock

When not to halve

Strokes are *not* halved if, as a result, the outline would be difficult to read:

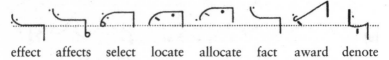

effect   affects   select   locate   allocate   fact   award   denote

An upward R, standing alone, is not halved for T or for D.
It would too closely resemble the shortforms *and* or *should*.
For example:

rate rates wrote rats rode/road

If a sounded vowel comes between R or L and D, halving is *not* used, and the full strokes are written:

erode payload corrode ballad charade

EXERCISE 11

(a)

(b)

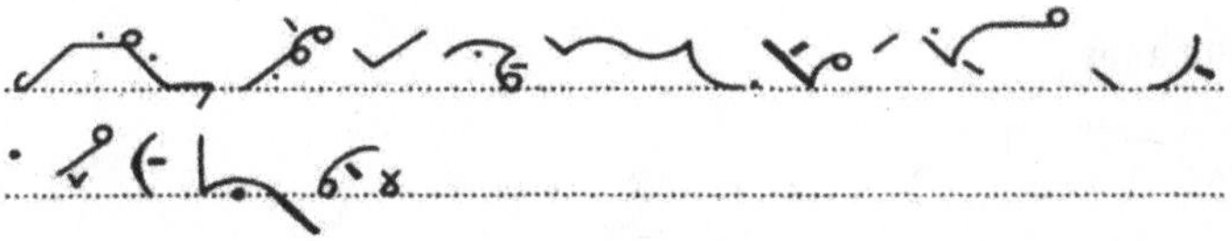

(c)

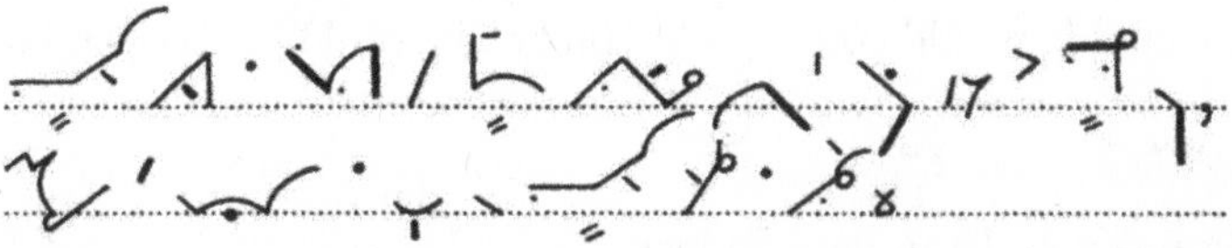

(d)

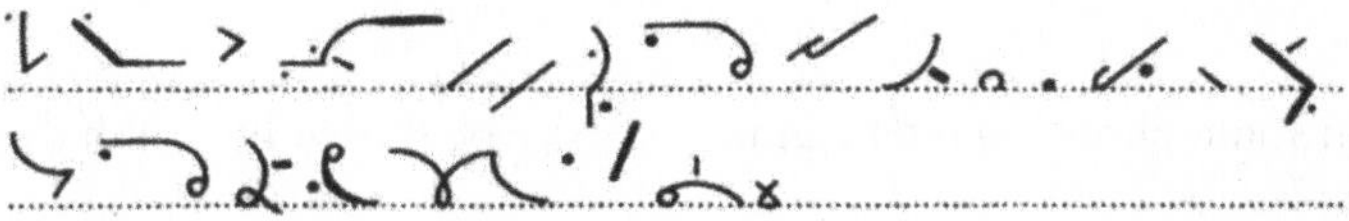

(e)

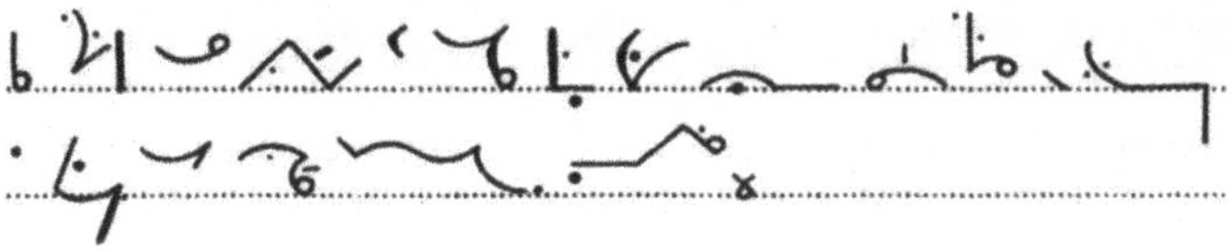

Full or half-length?

Make a clear distinction between a standard-length stroke and a half-length stroke. You are now using three lengths of stroke: standard, half-length and those even shorter ones in short forms like *and*, *on* and *of*.

SHORT FORMS

Copy and memorise:

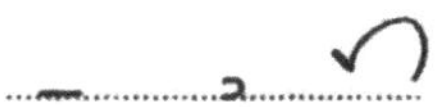

could   would   also

Notes:

(a) could *is a half-length K written on the line.*
(b) would *is a small light clockwise semicircle written on the line.*
(c) also *is formed from the vowel sound AW and L.*

Phrases

we could   would you   would you be   it would be   let you know

let us know let us have in fact

In some phrases *would* can more easily be shown by a W halved, as in:

I would   I would be   we would be   they would be

they would not be   this would

Omissions

Notice that in the phrase *in fact*, the consonant F is omitted. Omitting strokes from phrases is very common, as you will see.

EXERCISE 12

(a)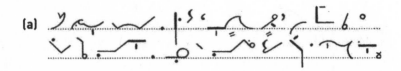

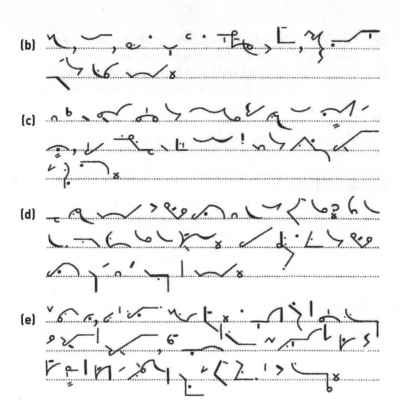

(b)

(c)

(d)

(e)

Clarity is everything

Write half strokes precisely, so that they are clearly different from normal length strokes, and only use them when there can be no mistake about their meaning.

EXERCISE 13

Write the following in shorthand, afterwards checking with the key (phrasing is indicated by hyphens):

(a) *I-met them at-the-same spot as-we-had met a month ago, but as I-was in-the car I-could fetch-the mats and carpets and load them on Tom's estate car.*

(b) *We-expected to-have a report today with-the results of-the work of-our firm in Canada, but-we-have-not had it yet.*

(c) *Select-the things you would care to purchase in-the pages of-the catalogue, make up-the Purchases-Form and-have it sent to-us today.*

(d) *Although our manufacturers have-not sent-us all-that-we asked for, I-think-we ought to manage at-this month's rates of sales.*

Dictation time

This exercise is present as dictations on the audio. Try Ex 16.A now, and then try Ex 13.B before going on to Unit 4.

THINGS TO REMEMBER

▶ *Any thin stroke can be halved to add T.*

▶ *Any thick stroke can be halved to add D.*

▶ *But don't halve if that would make the outline difficult to read.*

▶ *Circle S can be added to halved strokes.*

4

Common combinations

In this unit you will learn:
*   *how to show L by adding a hook to a stroke*
*   *about TL and DL endings*
*   *about INGS endings*

The L hook

Some groups of consonants commonly occur together in English words, and Pitman Shorthand provides abbreviating devices for these.

For example, a consonant followed by an L is of very frequent occurrence in English as in *pl*ate, *cl*aim, *bl*ame, nu*cl*eus, com*pl*icate, ena*bl*ing, and so on.

All the straight strokes (with the exception of R (up), W and Y – all for obvious reasons) may be initially hooked to add L as in:

P   PL   B   BL   K   KL   G   GL

T   TL   D   DL   CH   CHL   J   JL

Note that this L hook is always written to the left – anticlockwise.

It can be used in one of two ways:

1 *As a consonant, as in:* .... play .... tablet

2 *As a syllable, as in:* .... double .... tackle

Here are some examples:

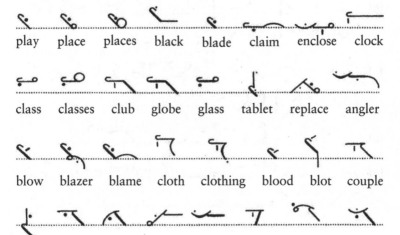

| play | place | places | black | blade | claim | enclose | clock |

| class | classes | club | globe | glass | tablet | replace | angler |

| blow | blazer | blame | cloth | clothing | blood | blot | couple |

| table | cable | label | circle | angle | cudgel | sample | enable |

local capable uncle ankle Naples

Think about the whole outline

Notice carefully that the L hook is added at the start of the stroke, though its sound comes after it. The position helps to produce clearer outlines that can be written faster, but it does point out the need to think about the whole outline before you start writing. If you try to write a shorthand outline in the same way that you write a word – letter by letter (or rather, sound by sound) – you can get into a mess.

EXERCISE 14

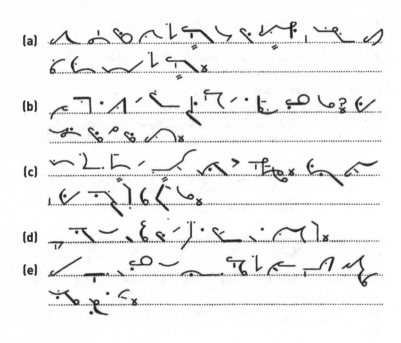

(a)

(b)

(c)

(d)

(e)

The final syllables -TL or -DL

Many words end with these syllables, though the spelling varies (*meddle, pedal, model, cattle, metal*). They are all written with the hooked T or the hooked D:

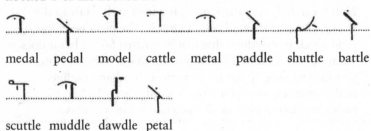

medal   pedal   model   cattle   metal   paddle   shuttle   battle

scuttle   muddle   dawdle   petal

The hook L is written small and round. The beginning of the hook should start parallel with the straight stroke. The hook should not be turned in towards the stroke, nor made angular.

L hook with circle S

S preceding the hooked stroke is written by tucking the circle inside the hook. This may be done initially or in the middle of an outline, as in:

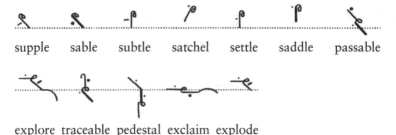

splash   exclaim

The circle S is kept very small and is more oval than circular when written inside the L hook.

Both the circle and the hook must be clearly shown when they occur in the middle of an outline.

Look carefully at these examples, then write them out yourself.

supple   sable   subtle   satchel   settle   saddle   passable

explore traceable pedestal exclaim explode

Plural -INGS

Where a word ending in -ING has been derived from a verb, the outline has a final dot to show the -ING. Such words may often be used as nouns, and so have a plural -INGS. This is shown by a short dash replacing the dot, as in:

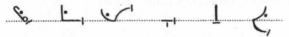

placings takings failings cuttings doings shavings

SHORT FORMS

Copy and memorise:

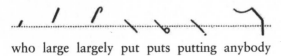

who large largely put puts putting anybody

Note: the short form for *who* is a short heavy downstroke.

Phrases

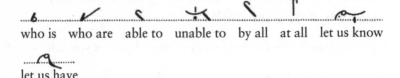

who is who are able to unable to by all at all let us know

let us have

EXERCISE 15

(a)

(b)
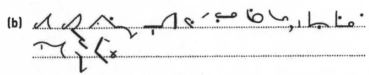

(c)

(d)

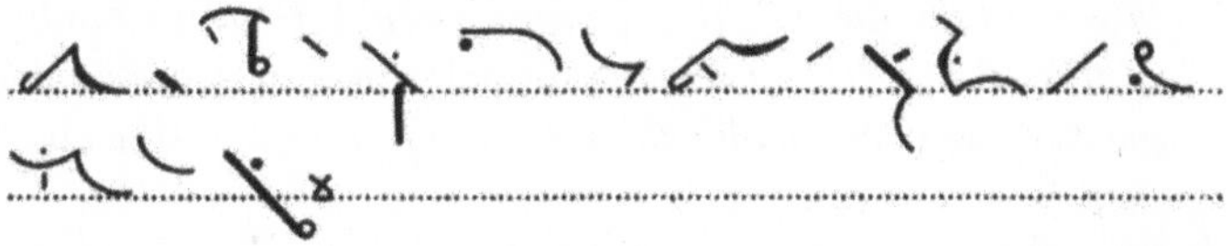

(e)

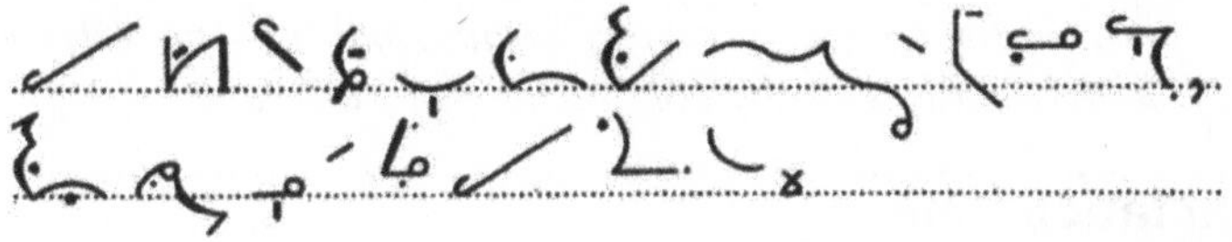

(f)

(g)

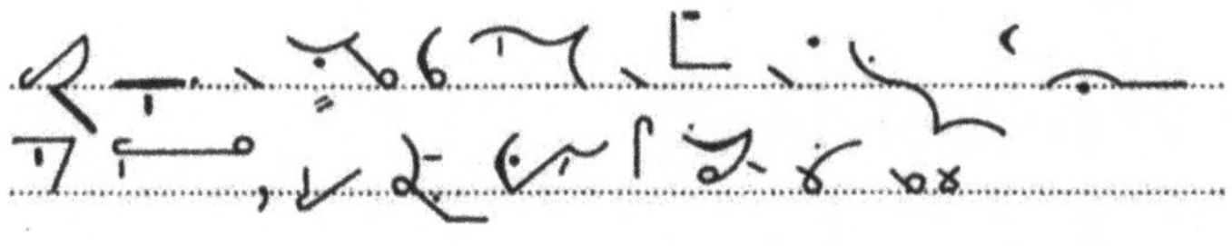

(h)

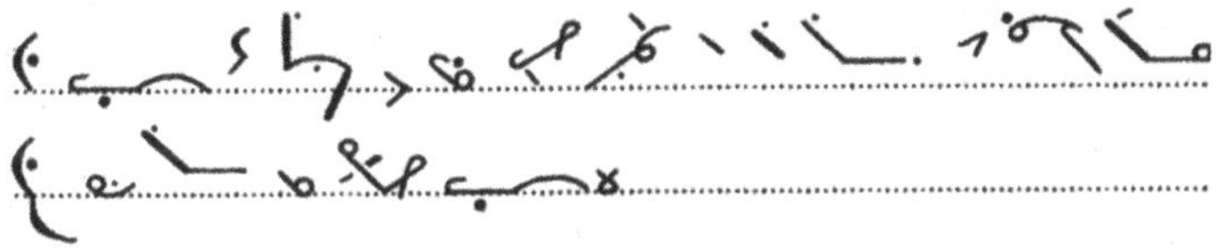

EXERCISE 16

Write the following in shorthand, afterwards checking with the key (phrasing is indicated by hyphens):

(a) *They said they-would-not-be coming at-all today, but they-have changed that and-we-are to-expect them at-the lodge as-it gets dark.*

(b) *We-have-not enough places at-the table for all of-them and so we-shall ask for a change of date and search for a spot with space for-them all.*

(c) *I-shall catch-the shuttle to Glasgow and be at-the Temple Bar Motel with an hour to spare, in-which I-shall settle up with-the firm we owe for-those sable furs they let-us-have in March.*

(d) *Uncle Jack told-us to put-the day's takings in-this black bag and take them in-the car to-the wall safe of-the bank in Market Road; but supposing for any cause we-were unable-to get-the bag in-the wall safe, we-were to-take it to-the club and wait.*

(e) *Our clerk rang some customers to-tell them that-they-would-not get-the cheques for a day or-two, and-that-this delay was largely because of-the bomb damage to-the bank.*

Dictation time

This exercise is included in the dictations on the audio.
Try Ex 16.A now, and then try Ex 13.B.

Review

Read, copy and then re-read from your own copy each of the four passages that follow.

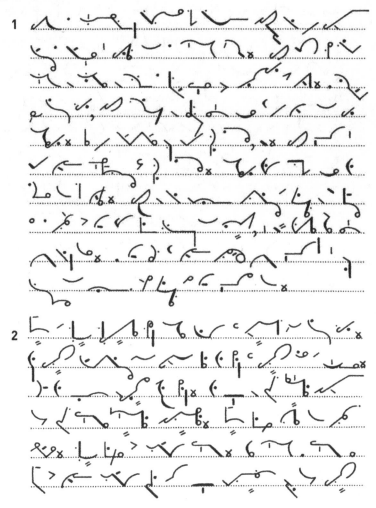

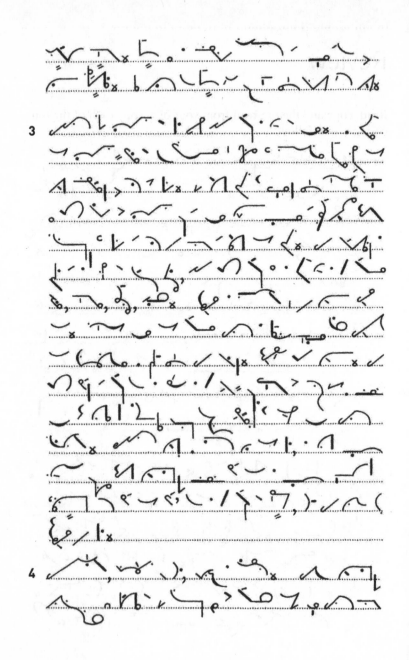

46

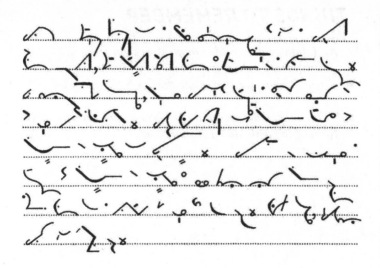

THINGS TO REMEMBER

▶ *An L hook can be added to most straight strokes.*

▶ *Circle S can be written inside the hook to add an initial S.*

▶ *With verbs, a dot will add the -ING ending. For the -INGS form of the verb, add a dash instead.*

5

Third-place vowels

In this unit you will learn:
* **the dots to represent ee sounds**
* **the dashes for oo sounds**

Dots

The vowels heard in the words *beet* and *bit* are represented by a heavy dot and a light dot respectively. These dots are placed before or after the stroke according to whether the vowels precede or follow the stroke, and the place for the vowel is read in the direction that the stroke is going.

L is an upward stroke so vowel-places are read .... as in the words:

...... ill ...... lee

D is a downward stroke so vowel-places are read .... as in the words:

...... Dee ...... did

N is a horizontal stroke from left to right so the vowel-places are read .... as in the words:

...... neat ...... knit

Two rules to remember

1 *When the first vowel in a word is a third-place vowel, the first upward or downward stroke is written through the line. If the outline consists only of horizontal strokes, then it is written on the line.*

2 *When a third-place vowel occurs between two consonants, it is written in the third place before the* second *consonant. (This keeps the vowel out of angles where it might be hard to write or read.)*

Look for these rules at work in the following examples:

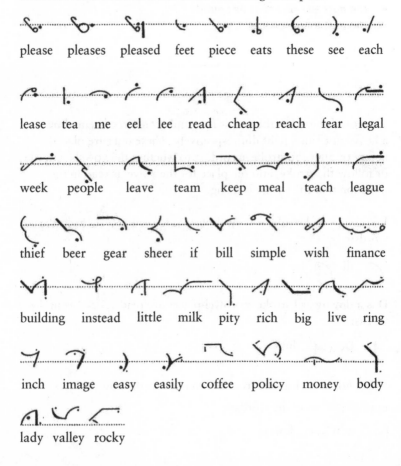

please   pleases   pleased   feet   piece   eats   these   see   each

lease   tea   me   eel   lee   read   cheap   reach   fear   legal

week   people   leave   team   keep   meal   teach   league

thief   beer   gear   sheer   if   bill   simple   wish   finance

building   instead   little   milk   pity   rich   big   live   ring

inch   image   easy   easily   coffee   policy   money   body

lady   valley   rocky

Dashes

The vowels heard in the words *food* and *book* are represented by
a heavy dash and a light dash respectively. They are placed as the
same way as the third-place vowel dots, as in:

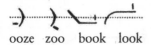

ooze   zoo   book   look

Remember the rule

When the first vowel in a word is a third-place vowel the
first upward or downward stroke is written through the line.
When a third-place vowel occurs between two consonants,
it is written before the second consonant:

Examples

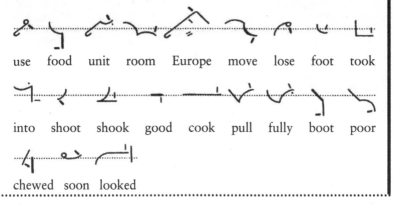

use   food   unit   room   Europe   move   lose   foot   took

into   shoot   shook   good   cook   pull   fully   boot   poor

chewed   soon   looked

Horizontal outlines

When the first vowel in the word is a third-place vowel, and the
outline has no upward or downward strokes, then the outline is
written on the line:

good   include   scheme   mini   nook   guinea   Mick

Get the right angle!

Notice how a dash vowel is always written at right angles to the stroke at the point at which it is written, for example:

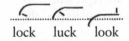

lock   luck   look

EXERCISE 17

(a)

(b)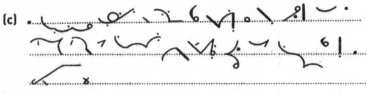

(c)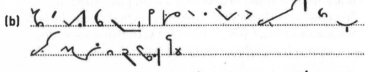

(d)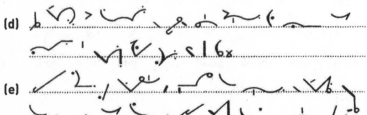

(e)

Only two this time!

year   Mrs

Intersections

The word *business* may, when convenient, be represented by striking a stroke B circle S through the last stroke of an outline, as in:

export business   your business   tomorrow's business

It is also possible for this or any other intersection to strike the stroke through at the beginning and thus indicate that the intersecting word comes first, as in:

business lunches   business affairs   business colleagues

This is also true of any other intersection, as in:

charge cards   form-filling

Phrasing

The phrase *to be* is represented by the single stroke for B written through the line: ......⟍.... to be.

Halving is used in various ways in phrasing. This is the first way: a stroke halved may add the word *it*, for example:

if   if it   I think   I think it

in which it is   I think it is

When convenient, the word *possible*  may be shortened by omitting the final syllables:

if it is possible   if it were possible   it is possible

Missing sounds

Omission of a word or of a syllable or of one sound is a common method used in phrasing and we shall meet many other examples.

EXERCISE 18

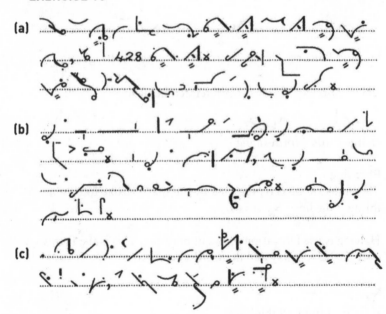

(a)

(b)

(c)

(d)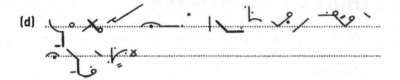

Get into position

Before you write an outline, think of the first vowel sound in the word and use that to position the stroke in relation to the line.

EXERCISE 19

Write the following in shorthand. Check your notes from the key, then re-write the exercise (phrasing is indicated by hyphenation):

(a) *This year we-shall-be publishing two books on Kenya, and-they-will both include articles on coffee, tea and cashew nuts, and, of-course, on safaris and-the game that roam in-the-parks.*

(b) *We-have managed to-get Sea Cottage on lease for a year and-we-are-pleased with-it. It-has ample space for-the six of-us and-the rooms are sunny and welcoming. It-has all-the facilities that-we-could wish for.*

(c) *I-have a scheme to-sell this mini this year and purchase an MG instead. But I-shall-have to-save to-get-the necessary money.*

(d) *This shop sells clothes and food, both of-them good, and it-has built up a large business in four years.*

(e) *We-are asking Mrs Cody to-go into Europe to build up our export-business in Italy and Germany.*

Dictation time

This exercise is included in the dictations on the audio.
Try Ex 19.A now, then Ex 16.B before going on to the next unit.

THINGS TO REMEMBER

▶ *There are only two symbols for the simple vowels – the dot and the dash, but they can be light or heavy. Make the difference between them clear.*

▶ *Light or heavy, dot or dash, still only gives you four signs, so their position along the stroke is crucial.*

▶ *Vowels are placed before or after the consonant stroke to which they relate.*

▶ *Where a vowel sits between two consonants, it is placed before the second.*

6

Complex vowel sounds

In this unit you will learn:
- *about the diphthongs vowel sounds*
- *about triphone vowels*
- *how to use the SES circle in the middle of words*

Diphthongs

A diphthong is a run-on combination of two vowel sounds.
You can hear four in the words of this sentence. Say it aloud,
and listen carefully to the underlined letters:

I enj<u>oy</u> l<u>ou</u>d m<u>u</u>sic

The shorthand for three of these and up. The fourth is a small
complete semicircle just like the *you* short-form.

The first two, *I* and *OI*, are small arrowheads, *I* pointing down and
OI to the right. They are both first-place symbols, as in:

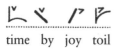

time   by   joy   toil

Ow is also a small arrowhead, pointing up, while YU is a small complete semicircle just like the *you* short-form. These are third-place symbols, as in:

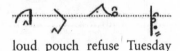

loud pouch refuse Tuesday

I diphthong

When a word starts with *I* ...., if it is immediately followed by a downstroke, the *I* is joined to it, writing the two together without a lift of the pen. An *I* sound following the consonant N is attached at the end of the N stroke:

eyes ice item isobar deny night nigh

Further examples

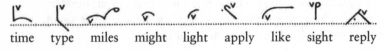

time   type   miles   might   light   apply   like   sight   reply

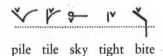

pile tile sky tight bite

OI diphthong

An initial OI before an L is joined to it, as in:

oil   oiling

Further examples

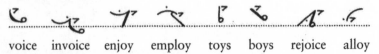

voice   invoice   enjoy   employ   toys   boys   rejoice   alloy

boil oiled annoy toil coils coiled

OW diphthong

If diphthong OW follows a downstroke and is the final sound
in the word it is joined to the stroke. If circle S follows, then the
diphthong sign cannot be joined:

bow/bough endow Chow vow thou bows

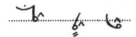

endows Chows vows

Straight downstrokes to which an OW can be joined may be
halved for T or D. When a circle S follows, however, the normal
halving rules hold.

Further examples

loud couch lounge county council outlaw allows blouse

ploughs cow sow endows rouse cloud

Halving one syllable words

Remember, in words of one syllable, light strokes may be
halved for T and heavy strokes for D.

bout doubt spout bouts doubts spouts

YU diphthong

If YU occurs at the end of a word the sign may be joined to downstrokes, but not if a circle S follows:

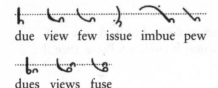

due view few issue imbue pew

dues views fuse

Single stroke outlines to which a YU can be joined may be halved for T or D, but normal halving rules apply when a circle S follows:

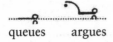

feud Bute feuds Bute's

After the consonants K, G, M, N and L, the YU diphthong may be turned and written anti-clockwise as shown:

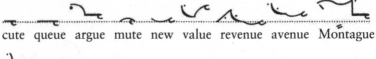

cute queue argue mute new value revenue avenue Montague

askew rescue

This cannot be done if circle S follows:

queues argues

Further examples

beauty bureau tubes music duke venue volume review

secure security news immunity unfortunate tunic

Triphones

Sometimes a third (unstressed) vowel is added to a diphthong. The sound is then called a *triphone*. It is shown by adding a tick to the diphthong:

science loyal tower fewer

EXERCISE 20

(a)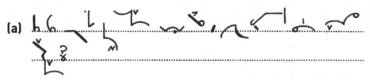

(b)

(c)

(d)

(e)

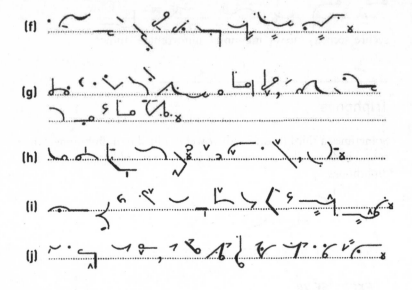

(f)

(g)

(h)

(i)

(j)

SES circle

In Unit 1, the SES circle was introduced as a large final circle for the plural of nouns already ending in S, as in:

..._O_.... guesses

and in the third person singular (he, she, it) of verbs ending in S, as in:

..._ß_.... rejoices ..._ÑO_.. revises

This large circle is often used in the middle or at the end of an outline, as in:

success possessive access accessible

If the vowel between the two Ss is a vowel or a diphthong other than E, then that is indicated by writing the vowel or diphthong in the circle. For dot vowels, a centrally placed light or heavy dot is written, and for dash vowels a light or heavy dash with an indication of the place of the vowel by sloping the inserted vowel as shown in the examples:

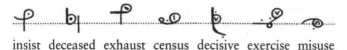

insist deceased exhaust census decisive exercise misuse

SHORT FORMS

To be copied and memorised:

should   without   influence   influenced influencing influences

several how now subject subjects subjecting subjected

Note: in .... now, the OW is shortened to a single stroke.

Writing notes

1 should *is written upward*.
2 without *is TH halved (like* that*).*

Standard endings apply

The short forms for the plurals, -ED and -ING words based on *influence* and *subject* follow the normal rules, so are very easy to learn.

Phrasing

Here are four more sets of phrases to learn.

1 *When I precedes K, G, M, W, L, upward R or a hooked downstroke, it is abbreviated to the first half of the short form only. For example:*

I came   I got   I am   I was   I will be   I am pleased

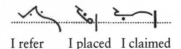

I refer   I placed   I claimed

2 *The word* time *in phrases:*

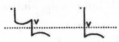

at any time   at a time (a is omitted)

at the same time (halving is used for the t)

for some time   at some time

3 *Some uses of the SES circle:*

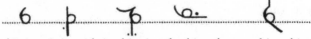

as soon as   as soon as we are able to   as soon as possible

this is   it is said   in this city   for his sake   on this subject

United States   United States of America

The SES circle is used alone for four phrases.

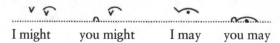

as is is as as has is his

Context makes it clear

You will see that the SES circle is used for four phrases.
Is this confusing? No. The position above or on the line
narrows down the options, but the context will usually make
the meaning clear.

4 I might *and* you might *are not written as phrases, to
distinguish them from* I may *and* you may:

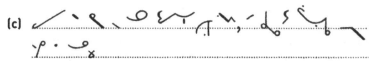

I might   you might   I may   you may

EXERCISE 21

Read, copy and re-read.

(a)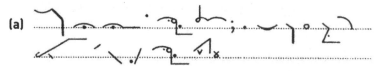

(b)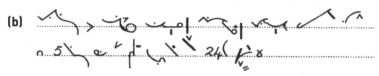

(c)

(d)

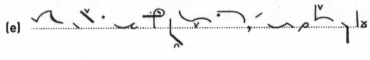

(e) ....

(f) ....

(g) ....

(h) ....

EXERCISE 22

Write the following exercise in shorthand. Check your notes from the key, and then re-write the exercise (phrasing is indicated by hyphenation):

(a) *I-have-no-doubt that at-some-time we ought to-meet to-discuss-the replies we-have received as a result of-our county survey.*

(b) *I-think-we should decide on-the venue of-the meeting right now, and discuss nothing else till that subject is settled.*

(c) *Joyce Lloyd has bought some space in-the local gazette to-tell people about-the beauty bureau she now has in-the market place.*

(d) *It-is-said that in-this-city about eight per cent of-the people are unemployed, but-we-are told that no boys or girls are among them.*

(e) *Sue Boyd has worked at-this job till she-is exhausted, and-is now lying on-the couch in-the lounge for an hour or-so.*

Dictation time

This exercise is included in the dictations on the audio.
Try Ex 22.A now, then try Ex 19.B before going on to
the next unit.

THINGS TO REMEMBER

▶ *In English there are four diphthong vowel sounds, I, OI, WO and YU.*

▶ *Three diphthongs are written as arrowheads, the fourth – YU – as a semi-circle.*

▶ *If a diphthong runs on to a third vowel, add a tick to the diphthong sign. This is a triphone.*

▶ *The large SES circle can be written in the middle of outlines.*

7

S and T in combinations

In this unit you will learn:
- *about the ST and STER loops*
- *how to add T and D to M or N*
- *different ways to show S and Z*
- *about diphone (double) vowel sounds*
- *two ways to show H*

S and T are so often used in combination with other letters that shorthand has special ways of dealing with the sounds.

The ST loop

The consonant combination ST is frequent in English, at the start, end and in the middle of words like *stock*, *last*, and *elastic*.

The sound of the ST combination is represented by a flat loop, half the length of the stroke to which it is written. The direction of writing the ST loop is the same as for circle S: anticlockwise to straight strokes, and always inside curves:

test   past   best   coast   guest   chest   just   stop   stock   stitch

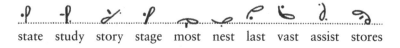

state   study   story   stage   most   nest   last   vast   assist   stores

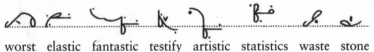

worst   elastic   fantastic   testify   artistic   statistics   waste   stone

Circle S may be added to an ST loop as shown:

test   tests   rusts   wastes   lists   nests   chests

In words like *worst* and *bursts*, a final R followed by a simple ST is written downwards:

worst   bursts

VOWELS AND ST

If a vowel precedes an initial ST, as in *astute* or if a vowel follows a final ST, as in *bestow*, then the ST loop cannot be used:

astute   bestow

If a vowel separates the S and the T, then circle S and stroke T are used:

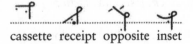

cassette   receipt   opposite   inset

The -STER loop

This is used when the sound combination of -STER is in the middle or at the end of words – not at the start. It is written with a loop similar to ST but much larger, two-thirds of the length of the stroke to which it is written.

Circle S can be added to -STER as shown:

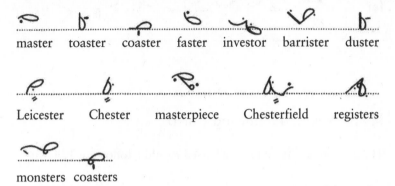

master   toaster   coaster   faster   investor   barrister   duster

Leicester   Chester   masterpiece   Chesterfield   registers

monsters   coasters

Writing note

The ST loop must be kept small and flat. The -STER loop
may be large, even slightly bulbous, as long as its size does
not affect the length of the stroke to which it is written.

EXERCISE 23

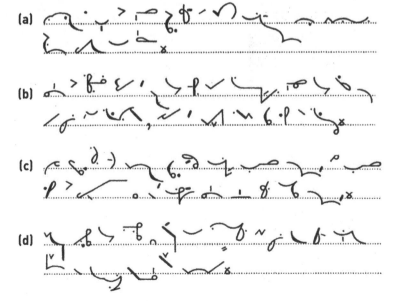

(a)

(b)

(c)

(d)

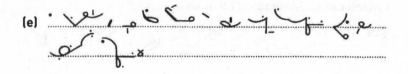

(e)

M and N with a following T or D

The consonants M and N are halved to add a following T, as in:

might meet note night

When they are halved to add a following D, they are thickened at the same time. They may be halved for D whether the word is a monosyllable or not. A vowel may be placed before the M or N, or between the M and D or the N and D:

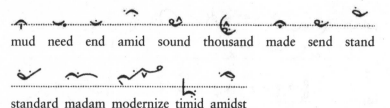

mud need end amid sound thousand made send stand

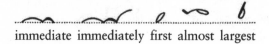

standard madam modernize timid amidst

SHORT FORMS

To be copied and memorized:

immediate immediately first almost largest

(Note that *first* is written anticlockwise.)

Phrasing

1 *We use the ST loop in phrases as follows:*

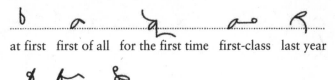

at first   first of all   for the first time   first-class   last year

just as   just now   as fast as

(Note that words are omitted in first of all *and* for the first time*)*

2 *By omitting the T and writing just a circle S we have a useful group of phrases:*

past year   past few years   must be   last time   post office

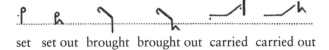

next week   in most cases   West Indies

3 *Other useful* time *phrases (see Phrasing 2 in Section 7) are:*

lunch time   spare time

4 *The word* out *can be shown in some phrases by halving the stroke that precedes it and adding the diphthong OU, as in:*

set   set out   brought   brought out   carried   carried out

Joining the loop to the stroke

The ST loop should join the stroke at its half-way point.

EXERCISE 24

(a)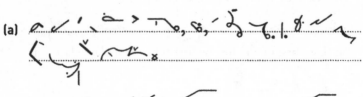

(b)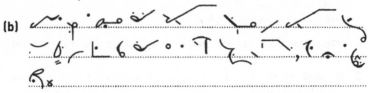

(c)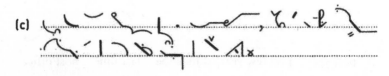

(d)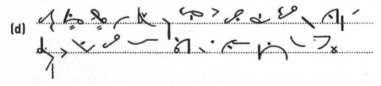

(e)

(f)

(g)

(h)

(i)

(j)

S and Z

There are two ways of representing the sound of S in shorthand –
by the small circle S and by the stroke, as in:

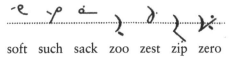

laws stay saw say

The small circle is used for S when it is the first sound in the word.
When the initial sound in a word is the harder Z (the voiced
consonant) then the heavy stroke ....)..... is used:

soft such sack zoo zest zip zero

In the middle or at the end of words, the circle S represents either the S or the Z sound:

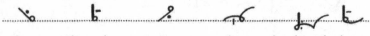

pays, pace   doze, dose   raise, race   muzzle, muscle   dismal   dozen

chisel   physical   visitor   user   chosen   raisin

When S or Z is the only consonant in the word then the thin S or thick Z stroke is used to match the sibilant sound. Strokes S and Z are shallow upright curves.

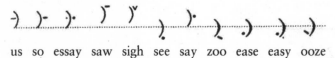

us   so   essay   saw   sigh   see   say   zoo   ease   easy   ooze

When S or Z is the first consonant in a word and is preceded by a vowel then the stroke is used:

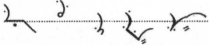

escape   assess   issue   Isabel   Islam

Similarly, when S or Z is the last consonant in a word and is followed by a vowel then the stroke is used:

legacy   lazy   accuracy   daisy   agency   rosy   policy

First and last strokes

Using a stroke for S or Z at the start or end of words where there is a vowel before or after gives us a way of indicating the presence or absence of a vowel without writing it, as in:

ask sack lass lasso

If the stroke S or Z is the first stroke in a root word then it is retained in derived words, as in:

ice icebox saw sawmill sea seaside

Diphones

There are a number of words in English in which one vowel is immediately followed by another without a consonant in between. For example, *radio* and *cooperate*. The two vowels in succession are called *diphones*, and are represented by a downward pointing sign, placed in the position of the first of the two vowels in the pair. This sign is often very helpful in making words instantly readable.

The diphone is an arowhead, written with a downward stroke on

the left, followed by an upward stroke on the right: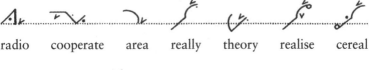

radio   cooperate   area   really   theory   realise   cereal

borrower jewelry ideal video serious medium

Diphthongs and diphones

There is a difference between these! In a diphthong (I, OI, OW, YU), the two vowel sounds form a single syllable. In a diphone, they are distinct sounds and make two syllables.

EXERCISE 25

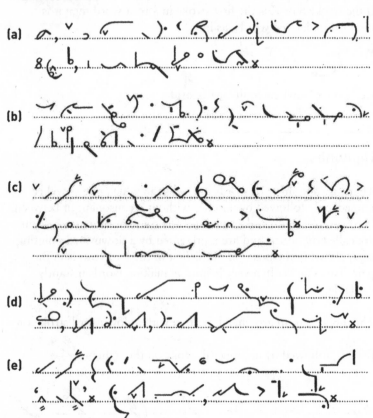

(a)

(b)

(c)

(d)

(e)

ZH

This spelling is conventionally used for the sound heard in such words as *garage*, *usual*, *visual*, *azure*, etc. The sound is the voiced form of SH, and is written in the same way, as a quarter circle, but with a heavier line:

usual usually azure garage visual casual Raj

H

STROKE H

The usual way to write H is with this stroke ..⌒.. which begins with a clockwise circle and ends with a straight line written upwards at an angle.

H is often an initial consonant, but it frequently appears in the middle of words:

happy hope high he haze hang hurry head heavy

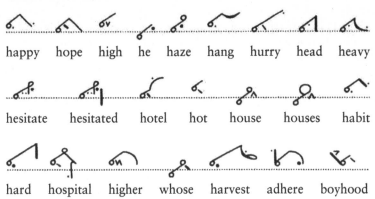

hesitate hesitated hotel hot house houses habit

hard hospital higher whose harvest adhere boyhood

unhappy upholster clubhouse rehearsal

Sahara seahorse Soho

If an H is not sounded in a word, then it is not written in the shorthand, as in:

exhume vehicle

When H immediately follows an S in the middle of a word, it is omitted – even though it is sounded:

falsehood household leasehold mishap

Only in the middle

The 'no H after S' rule only applies in the middle of words. Look at *Sahara*, *seahorse* and *Soho* at the end of the first set of examples.

TICK H

When H is the first consonant and the next is M or L or downward R, then H is written by a short downward tick from right to left known as tick H, as in:

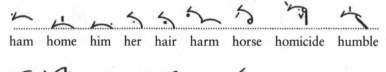

ham home him her hair harm horse homicide humble

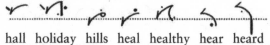

hall holiday hills heal healthy hear heard

One-syllable H-RT words are written with tick H and downward R halved:

heart hurt

If a downward R is used in a root word, it is retained in words derived from it:

hearty hurting hereby herself hoarsely

When tick H is used at the start of a word, before M, L and R down, it is short and slopes slightly from right to left.

hammock

Writing notes

Look carefully at the difference between H and S plus upward R, and between H and CH plus circle S.

hoe sorry hay chase

SHORT FORMS

Just two to remember this time!

anyhow New York

Phrasing

1 *In commonly-used phrases, the word* hope  *may be represented by the stroke P alone, omitting the H:*

I hope we hope we hope that you will we hope you are

2 *The usual way to write* he is 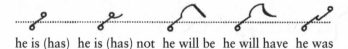 *. This is used when* he is *the first word in the phrase:*

he is (has)   he is (has) not   he will be   he will have   he was

When he *is in the middle or at the end of the phrase, it can be written – if it is convenient to do so, with a short heavy vertical downstroke, as in:*

if he is   if he is not   as he is   we think he will

we know that he is   if he were

3 *Note the use of tick H in the phrase:*

how much

4 *The tick H may be used in the middle of phrases such as:*

for whom   for himself

EXERCISE 26

(a)

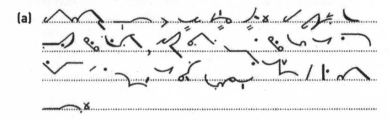

(b)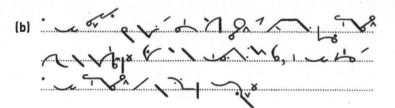

(c)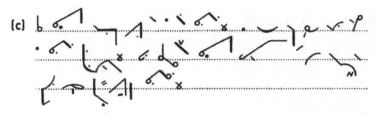

(d)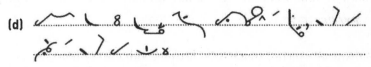

(e)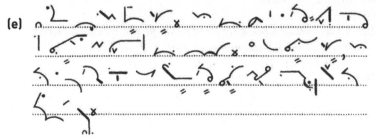

(f)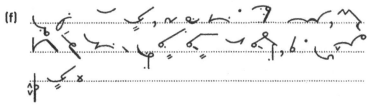

(g)

(h)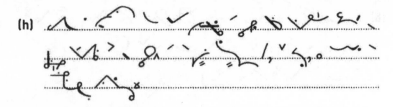

EXERCISE 27

Write in shorthand, afterwards checking with the key (phrasing is indicated by hyphens):

(a) *Please-make a booking for two single rooms at-the Home Farm Hotel for-the nights of 24th and 25th August in-the names of Mr Tom Hall and Mr Harry Hilary.*

(b) *The whole household was in a state of chaos at-the-time we arrived, and-this-was because a water pipe had burst and inundated-the downstairs rooms.*

(c) *He wrote an essay on 'The Zoos of-Europe', and it-was so good that-they sent him a cheque to allow it to-be published in-the Daily Gazette.*

(d) *It-is cold and-icy here on-the hills outside-the, city, and it-has stayed below zero all day. We-are lucky because-we-have a hot log fire in-the lounge of-the hotel to-keep-us warm.*

(e) *We usually start work in-the garage early in-the day and-we-have to hurry to-get all-the day's jobs ended by five o'clock.*

THINGS TO REMEMBER

▶ *Add a flat loop to an outline to show the ST and STER sounds.*

▶ *M and N can be halved to add T or D.*

▶ *S and Z as mainly written as circles, but strokes should be used where you need to show vowels.*

▶ *To show a diphone (double vowel sound) use a tick in place of the first vowel of the pair.*

▶ *H can be written as a stroke or as a tick.*

8

The R hook

In this unit you will learn:
- **when and how to add the R hook to straight strokes**
- **about circles and loops with R**
- **about stress in words**

R hook on straight strokes

Each of the simple straight strokes may be written with a small round hook at the beginning to add an R. The hook is written in a clockwise direction before starting the stroke:

\\ \\ | | / / ___ ___
P   B   T   D   CH   J   K   G

\\ \\ | | / / ___ ___
PR   BR   TR   DR   CHR   JR   KR   GR

These consonant combinations are very common in English, not only at the beginning of words, but also in the middle:

At the start:

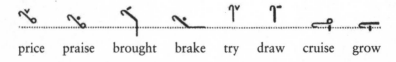

price   praise   brought   brake   try   draw   cruise   grow

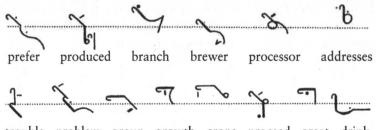

prefer   produced   branch   brewer   processor   addresses

trouble   problem   group   growth   crops   proceed   great   drink

In the middle:

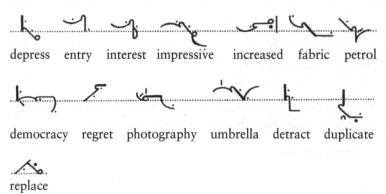

depress   entry   interest   impressive   increased   fabric   petrol

democracy   regret   photography   umbrella   detract   duplicate

replace

The R hook can also be used for the syllables AR, ER and OR.

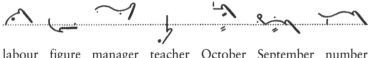

labour   figure   manager   teacher   October   September   number

ledger   water   actor   banker   shippers   vigour   sugar

In the middle of an outline, if circle S precedes an R hook to a straight stroke, the circle is also written clockwise. This helps to show both the circle and the hook clearly, as in:

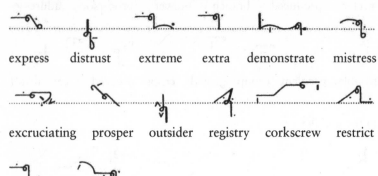

express   distrust   extreme   extra   demonstrate   mistress

excruciating   prosper   outsider   registry   corkscrew   restrict

extricate   orchestra

In other cases, the circle S can be merged with the R hook, and we will return to this after the next exercise.

EXERCISE 28

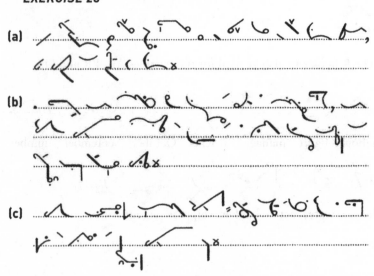

(a)

(b)

(c)

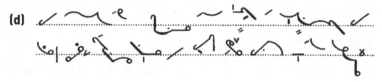

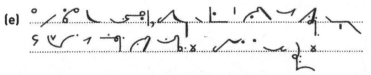

The R hook and the L hook

The hooks to straight strokes must be written small and round. The R hook is written round to the Right (clockwise), the L hook to the Left.

CIRCLES AND LOOPS TO R HOOKS TO STRAIGHT STROKES

A circle S is written to an R hook to a straight stroke by simply closing the hook, as in:

STR   SPR   SKR

Vowels may come between the S and the initial hook, as in:

setter sober cider seeker

The STR, SPR, SKR combinations of consonants may be followed by vowels, as in:

stress   spring   screws   straight   strong   scratch

struck   straw   strange

When SKR, SGR follows ....|.. D, ...\.. P or ....\.. B both hook and circle are show:

disgrace describe prescribe subscribe discriminate

In a word beginning with S plus R hook to a straight stroke, vowels may come between the S and the R hook and after the R hook, as in:

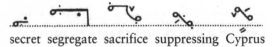

secret segregate sacrifice suppressing Cyprus

The ST loop may be used in a similar way by writing it clockwise to the hooked stroke:

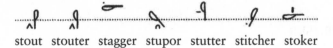

stout stouter stagger stupor stutter stitcher stoker

EXERCISE 29

(a) [shorthand outlines]

(b) [shorthand outlines]

(c) [shorthand outlines]

(d)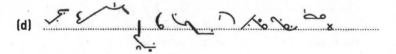

Stress rules

We now have two initial hooks to straight strokes, the L hook and the R hook. Both of these hooks may be used as consonants, as in .... *place* and .... *press*, or as a syllable, as in .... *people* and .... *papers*.

The stress rules control when hooks may be used as syllable and when they may not. Almost every English word that has two syllables or more has a firm stress on one of them, i.e. one syllable is spoken more firmly and loudly than the rest. For example, in the word *para̲lyse* the stress is on the first of the three syllables. In *infor̲mer* the stress is on the second syllable, and in *engineer̲* it is on the third syllable.

1 *If the first syllable is unstressed, the rule is that any initially hooked stroke may be used to represent syllables, no matter what vowel comes between stroke and hook. For example, in the words per̲form, por̲tray, coll̲ect and cur̲tail, the hooked forms may be used for all the first syllables because they are unstressed, and so we write:*

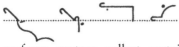

perform   portray   collect   curtail

On the other hand, in the words such as <u>pur</u>pose, <u>bar</u>ley, <u>cal</u>orie and <u>corr</u>idor the first syllable is stressed. We cannot use the hooked form for these, and so we write:

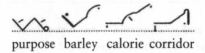

purpose barley calorie corridor

2 *In words of one syllable only, the initially hooked form may not be used:*

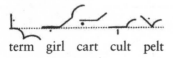

term girl cart cult pelt

3 *The form is used in a root word is retained in derivatives even though the stressed syllable may change, as in:*

territory territorial participle participial

Exceptions

These stress rules can be ignored if doing so will produce a more readable or more easily written outline, e.g.:

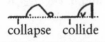

collapse collide

SHORT FORMS

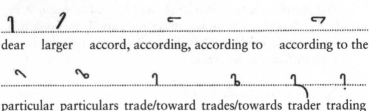

dear larger accord, according, according to according to the

particular particulars trade/toward trades/towards trader trading

92

Intersections

A consonant K may be struck through another stroke to indicate the word *company*:

transport company   shipping company   your company

Consonants K and L may be struck through another stroke to indicate *company limited*:

The Paper Company   The Wholemeal Loaf
      Limited   Company Limited

Phrasing

Dear Sir Dear Madam yours faithfully yours truly yours sincerely

Notice the word *course*. As this is a monosyllable it is normally written, following the stress rule. However, in a phrase the hooked form is used.

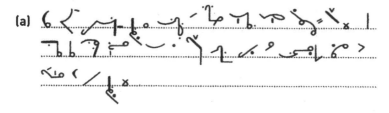

of course   in due course

EXERCISE 30

(a)

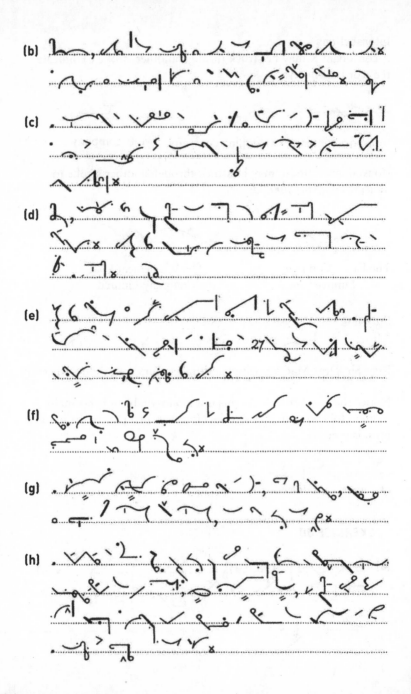

94

Write in shorthand, afterwards checking with the key (phrasing is indicated by hyphens):

Dear-Sir,

You were correct in assuming that-we should-be collecting your household goods and-effects in-the coming week, and-we-hope-that Thursday will-be a good day for-you. I-regret that-we-are-unable-to promise an exact time for arriving at-your new home because, of-course, of possible highway and-transport problems. As-we ought-to-be loaded by ten o'clock, I-think-it-is probable that-we-shall arrive by four o'clock and so we-shall still have some hours of-light for work.

Yours-faithfully,

Dictation time

This exercise is included in the dictations on the audio. Try Ex 31.A now, then try Ex 27.B before going on to the next unit.

Review

Read, copy, and then re-read from your own copy each of the
four passages that follow. Then re-transcribe them back into
the shorthand from the key without reference to your original
shorthand.

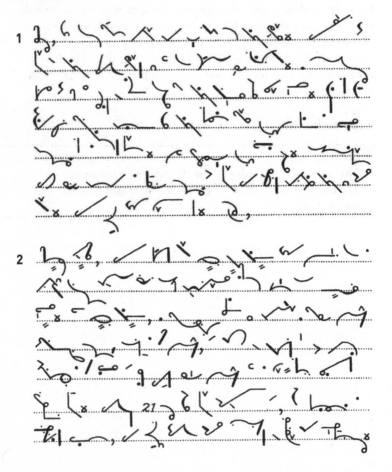

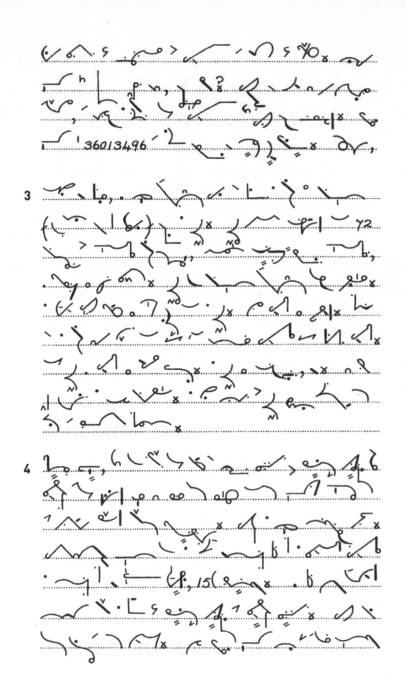

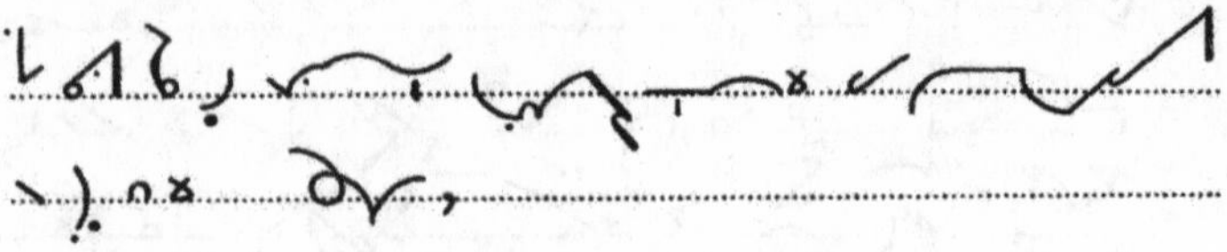

THINGS TO REMEMBER

▶ *Hooks can only be used for unstressed first syllables, and not at all on one-syllable words.*

▶ *R hooks to straight strokes are written to the Right.*

▶ *L hooks are written to the Left.*

▶ *An initial S can be added by closing the hooks.*

Hook N

In this unit you will learn:
- *how to write hook N to curved strokes*
- *and to straight strokes*
- *when you can use hook N in the middle of a word*

Final hook N to curved strokes

The sound of N at the end of a word is very common in English. When N is the last sound and is not followed by a vowel, a small round hook is used to represent it. This can be written to every one of the 24 consonants.

At the end of a curved stroke, the N hook is written inside the curve, for example:

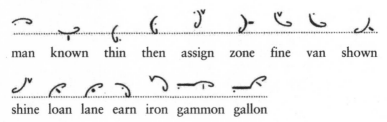

man   known   thin   then   assign   zone   fine   van   shown

shine   loan   lane   earn   iron   gammon   gallon

At the end of a straight stroke, it is written clockwise:

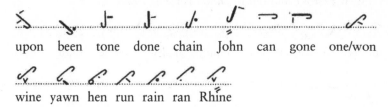

upon been tone done chain John can gone one/won

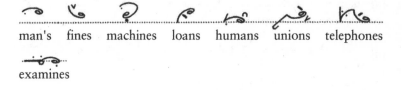

wine yawn hen run rain ran Rhine

Writing notes

The final hook N must be written small and round. It is a
small semicircle.

A circle S may be tucked inside the final hook N when they make
an -NZ sounds, as in:

man's fines machines loans humans unions telephones

examines

When the final sounds after a curved stroke are -NS or -NSES,
then a stroke and a circle are used:

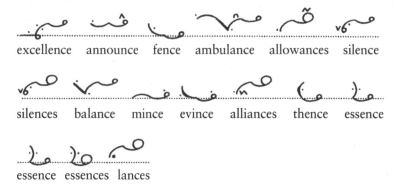

excellence announce fence ambulance allowances silence

silences balance mince evince alliances thence essence

essence essences lances

When there is a vowel between a final N and S or Z or after a final N, then a stroke and not the hook is used:

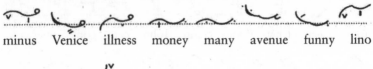

minus   Venice   illness   money   many   avenue   funny   lino

Ernie   nanny   shyness

Finishing with a vowel

A final vowel must always have a final stroke.

EXERCISE 32

(a)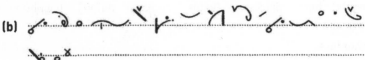

(b)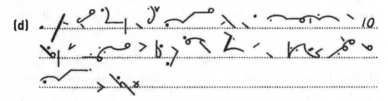

(c) ...

(d) ...

(e)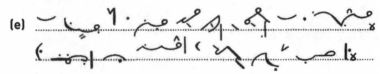

In any words ending in NT or ND sounds, a curved stroke may take a hook for the N, then be halved to show T or D.

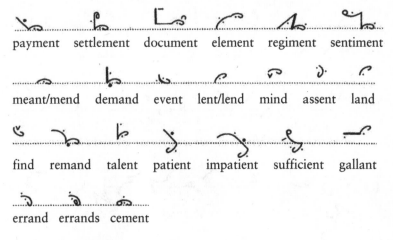

payment   settlement   document   element   regiment   sentiment

meant/mend   demand   event   lent/lend   mind   assent   land

find   remand   talent   patient   impatient   sufficient   gallant

errand   errands   cement

N IN THE MIDDLE

You should normally use a stroke not a hook for N in the middle of a word, as in:

finance   arrange   tenant   fancy   finish   vanish

The exception to this rule is when the word is a compound, and a final N hook was used in a root word. For example:

Root words:

man   land   moon

Compound words:

manpower   landlord   moonbeam

EXERCISE 33

(a)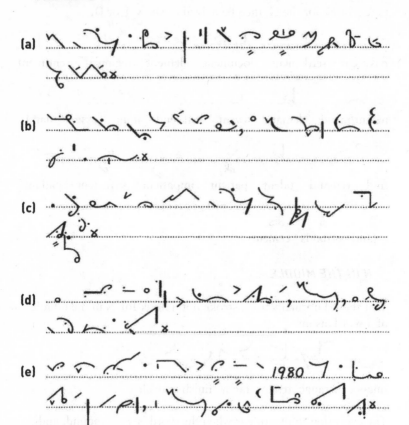

(b)

(c)

(d)

(e) 1980

nb.

SHORTFORMS

particularly   accordingly

Notice that the -LY has been disjoined in these. This is to make it clear that -LY has been added to simpler short forms.

Intersections

A downward R struck through a stroke represents *arrange* or *arranged* or *arrangement*. To this can be added a circle S to represent *arrangements*; or a dot -ING to give *arranging*:

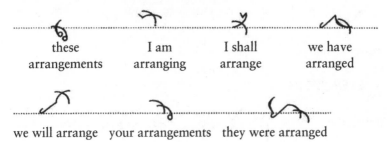

| these arrangements | I am arranging | I shall arrange | we have arranged |

we will arrange   your arrangements   they were arranged

PHRASING

1   ⎯⎯ *is the outline used for* business man. *A vowel is*

   inserted for business men ⎯⎯.

2   *In Section 3 the phrase* in fact *was given, showing that a consonant may be omitted so as to give an easy-to-read and easy-to-write outline. There were more examples of consonant omission in Unit 7, including such phrases as:*

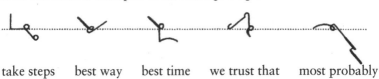

   past year   must be   last time   post office   next time   in most cases

Here are further examples of the same principle:

take steps   best way   best time   we trust that   most probably take care   family life   Prime Minister   in fact   of the fact that

better results

EXERCISE 34

(a)

(b)

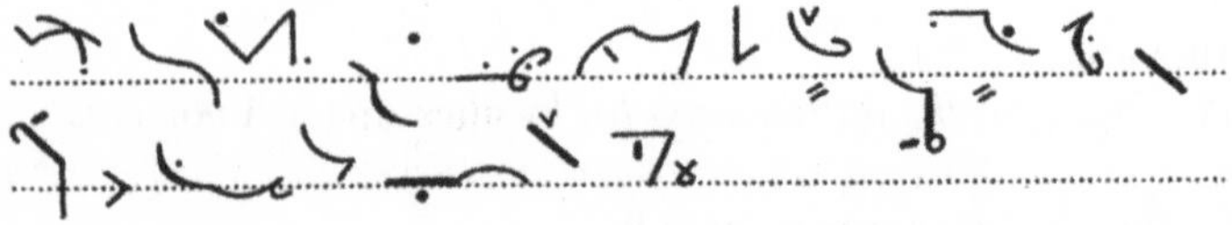

(c)

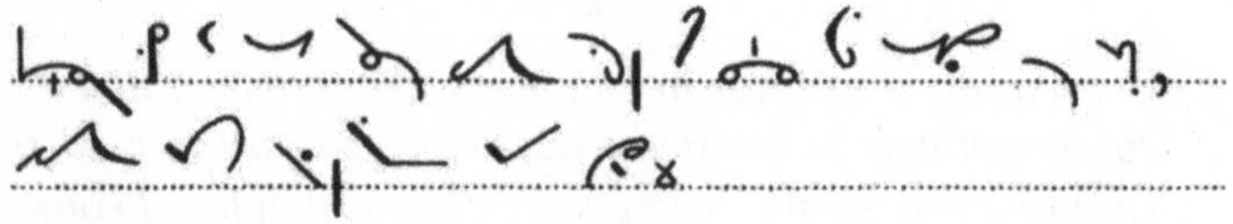

(d)

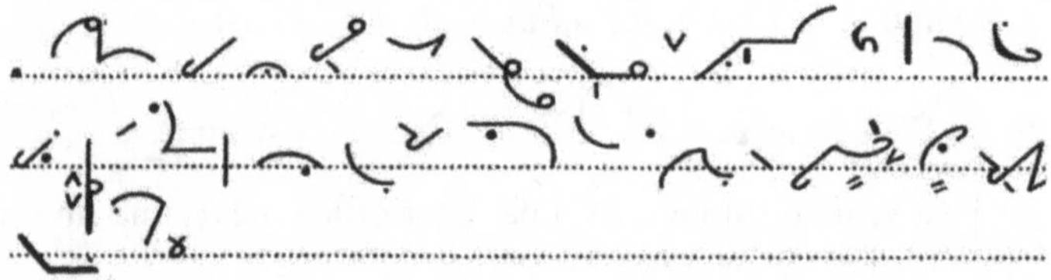

(e)

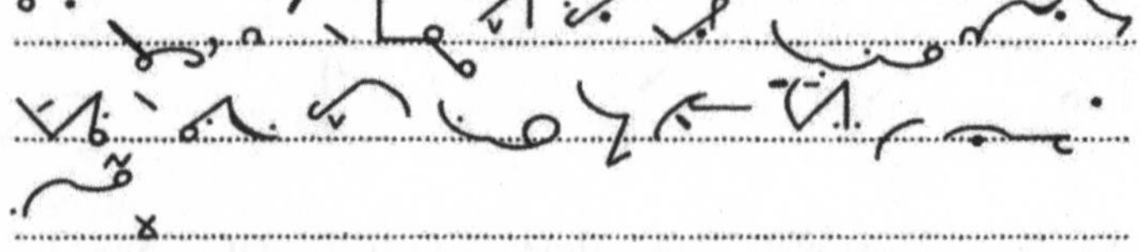

(f)

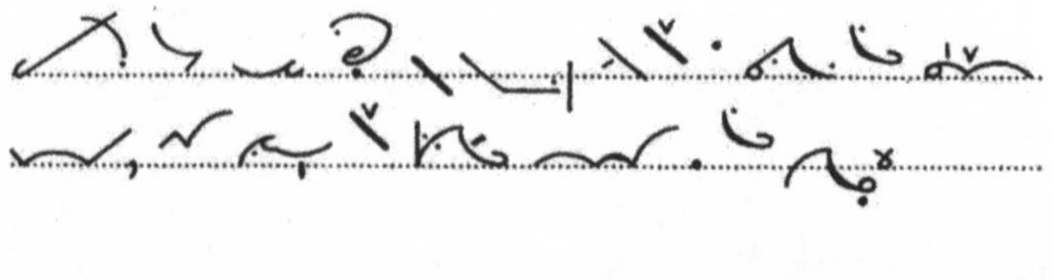

(g)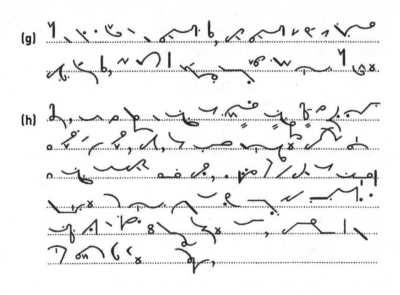

(h)

Final N hook to straight strokes

When a word ends in the sound of N and the preceding consonant
is a straight stroke, this is hooked for N. The N hook is a small
round semi-circle hook added to the straight stroke and written
clockwise:

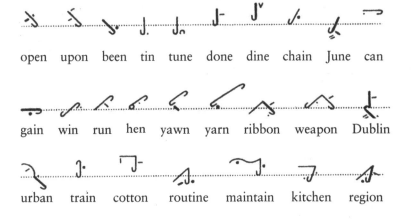

open upon been tin tune done dine chain June can

gain win run hen yawn yarn ribbon weapon Dublin

urban train cotton routine maintain kitchen region

screen begin foreign adjourn turn return

To add -S, -Z, -SES, -ST or -STER to the N hook, complete the circle, writing clockwise:

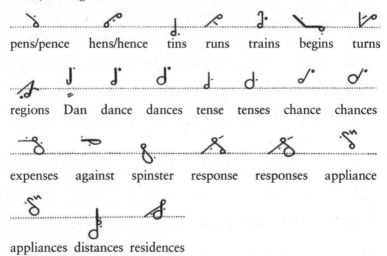

pens/pence   hens/hence   tins   runs   trains   begins   turns

regions   Dan   dance   dances   tense   tenses   chance   chances

expenses   against   spinster   response   responses   appliance

appliances   distances   residences

The direction counts

The direction of the circles or loops includes the N hook. You can see the difference in these examples:

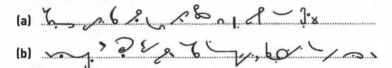

does   dunce   August   against   choices   chances

EXERCISE 35

(a)

(b)

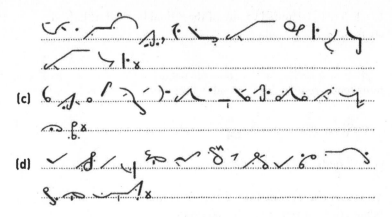

Any final straight stroke hooked for N may also be halved to add either T or D:

tend/tent Kent spend/spent second pound important extent

hand distant assistant assistance depend dependant

accident paint joint

R upward, when alone, cannot be halved for T because of possible

confusion with *and* or *should*. So we write 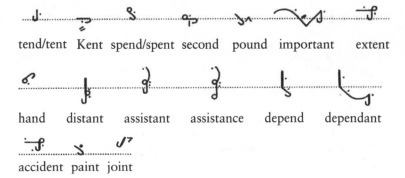 rates, roots etc. However, R upward when hooked for N may be halved to add T or D:

rent surround round rented surrounded rounded

Circle S may be added to any of these final hooked or halved strokes:

tents/tends rents/rends spends seconds hands assistants

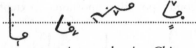

corresponds correspondence

You must use stroke N, for a final N is followed by a vowel, e.g. *penny*, or by a vowel and S, e.g. *bonus*.

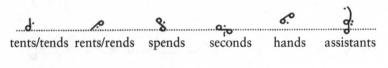

penny deny Tony tiny honey rainy bonus weakness

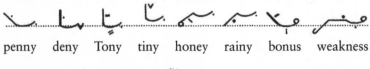

tetanus genius modernise Chinese

An N in the middle of a word is normally written with a stroke. Only use hook N for compound words, where the first word is written with hook N. For example, in bandsaw the root word band is written with a final N hook:

band bandsaw

If the two root words cannot be joined easily, then they are disjoined, the second part being written close up to the first:

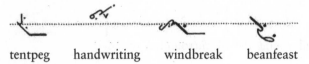

tentpeg handwriting windbreak beanfeast

brainstorm   train bearer

EXERCISE 36

(a)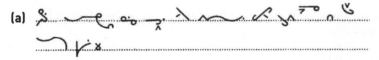

(b)

(c)

(d)

(e)

SHORT FORMS

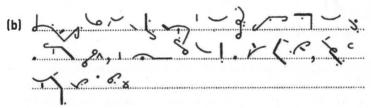

cannot responsibility anyone gentleman gentlemen

Intersections

A stroke D can be intersected for *department*:

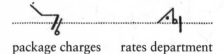

sales department   accounts department   welfare department

Any intersection can be written early in the outline, so that it is read first:

department heads   business rates

An intersection cannot be used if the stroke runs in the same direction as the final stroke of the preceding outline. In these cases, it can be written close up, as long as the meaning remains clear:

package charges   rates department

PHRASING

1 *The principle of halving a stroke finally hooked for N to add T or D is used to add* not *in such phrases as:*

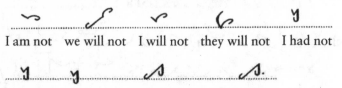

I am not   we will not   I will not   they will not   I had not

I do not   I did not   we do/had not   we did not

2 *If joined to a previous stroke, the same can be done for* are not, *as in:*

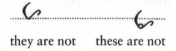

they are not   these are not

By itself, *are not* is written in full. ....~........

Note the special and very useful phrase *at once*. ....♩........

3 *Other phrases which have a final hook:*

....

I want I cannot we cannot it is certain

4 *At the end of a phrase, a final hook N may be used for* been, own, than *and* on. *Many such phrases can be formed. Here are some common ones:*

....

I had been   we have been   already been   your own   our own

....

her own   better than   smaller than   higher than   bigger than

....

easier than   carry on   carried on

The full outline for own .... is used in the phrases *my own* and *his own*, and whenever *own* follows stroke M or N.

....

my own   his own

EXERCISE 37

(a) ....

....

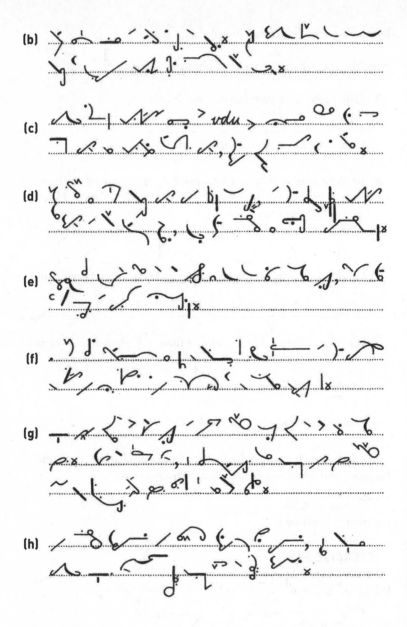

Write in shorthand, afterwards checking with the key (phrasing is indicated by hyphens):

Dear-Miss Jones,

I-am-not able-to see-you on-Monday, 20th June, but I-can-arrange-the second date you suggested, 27th June. I-hope-you-are-not now engaged for-that day, as-it-is urgent that-we decide-the amount of assistance that-you-will-need to-get-the task done by-the end of August. It-is-important, too, that-we-do-not-have to ask for-the time to-be extended longer-than that. So I-am ready to-be as liberal as I-can in paying for-the right kind of assistance. Will 11 am on-Monday, 27th June suit-you?

Yours-sincerely,

Dictation time

This exercise is included in the dictations on the audio, try Ex 38.A now. To help fix your earlier learning, try Ex 31.B.

THINGS TO REMEMBER

▶ A hook can be written at the end of a stroke to show a final N in a word.

▶ With curved strokes, the hook is written inside the curve

▶ With straight strokes, the hook is written clockwise

▶ An N hook can be used in the middle of an outline, but only with compound words

10

Suffixes and compounds

Suffixes

In this unit you will learn:
- *about the suffixes -MENT, MENTAL and -LY*
- *about the downward L stroke and when to use it*
- *about the suffixes -MENT, MENTAL and -LY*

A suffix is an ending which can be tagged on to a word to extend or change its meaning. English has a number of very common suffixes, e.g.:

- ▶ *care, careless, careful, carefulness;*
- ▶ *account, accountable, accountability;*
- ▶ *comrade, comradeship;*
- ▶ *myth, mythological;*
- ▶ *zoo, zoological.*

Shorthand treats some of these suffixes in a special way.

-MENT

-MENT is a very common suffix. It is usually written with M hooked for N and halved for T, as in:

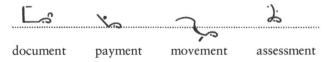

| document | payment | movement | assessment |

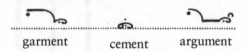

garment   cement   argument

When it is difficult or not possible to write -MENT this way, then
it can be represented by stroke N halved for T.

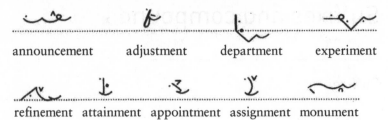

announcement   adjustment   department   experiment

refinement   attainment   appointment   assignment   monument

(It will be noted that in words formed from roots written with
final N hook, the hook is retained when the -MENT is added)

DIVERSION: DOWNWARD L

Before we look at other suffixes, you need to know another way
to write L.

L is normally written upward. However, when L immediately
follows stroke N, or stroke N halved, or stroke NG, it is always
written downward:

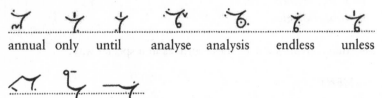

annual   only   until   analyse   analysis   endless   unless

wrongly   strongly   kingly

EXERCISE 39

(a)

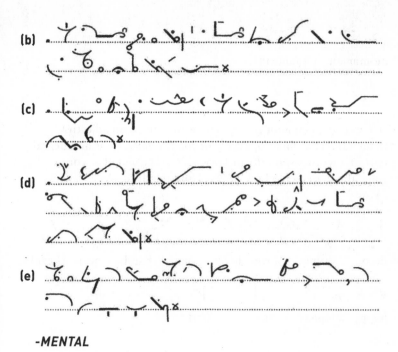

(b) ....

(c) ....

(d) ....

(e) ....

-MENTAL

The ending -MENTAL can be written in two ways. If the -MENT version of the word is written with M hooked for N and halved for T, then the M and N are changed to full strokes:

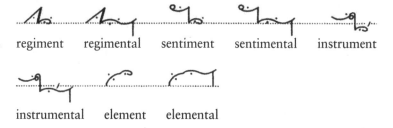

regiment   regimental   sentiment   sentimental   instrument

instrumental   element   elemental

If a word is written with N halved to represent -MENT, then downward L is added for the ending -MENTAL:

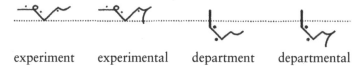

experiment   experimental   department   departmental

monument   monumental

-LY

-LY is a very common ending, either to convert an adjective
to an adverb, as in *deep*, *deeply* or *total*, *totally*, or as an integral
part of a word, as in *rally* or *holy*. -LY at the end of a word is
generally represented by L upward and the third-place short
I vowel:

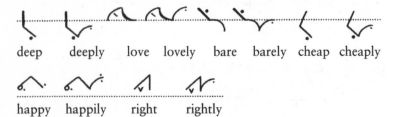

deep   deeply   love   lovely   bare   barely   cheap   cheaply

happy   happily   right   rightly

When a root outline ends with a hook N, this is retained in the -LY
word derived from it. If necessary, the -LY is disjoined:

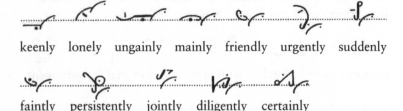

keenly   lonely   ungainly   mainly   friendly   urgently   suddenly

faintly   persistently   jointly   diligently   certainly

With words that have outlines ending with either an upward or
downward L, we form the -LY ending by inserting the third place
short I vowel:

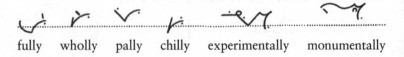

fully   wholly   pally   chilly   experimentally   monumentally

departmentally

We also show the -LY by inserting the third-place short I vowel when a root outline is written with a final stroke hooked for L:

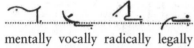

physical physically total totally topically locally logically

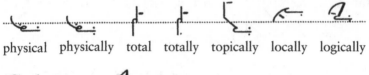

mentally vocally radically legally

To show the ending -LY after N or N halved or NG we use downward L with the third-place short I vowel:

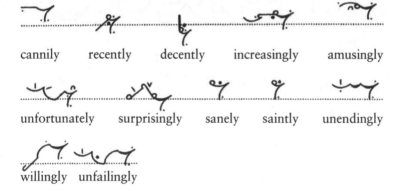

cannily   recently   decently   increasingly   amusingly

unfortunately   surprisingly   sanely   saintly   unendingly

willingly unfailingly

In some polysyllabic words, the ending is -ALLY, rather than -LY. This is represented by the final stroke hooked for L with the third-place short vowel I:

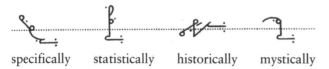

specifically   statistically   historically   mystically

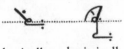

basically   logistically

EXERCISE 40

(a)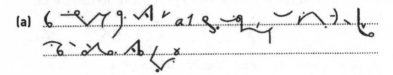

(b)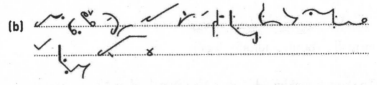

(c)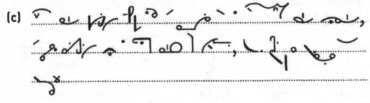

(d)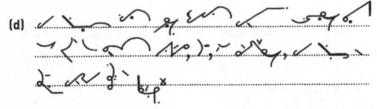

(e)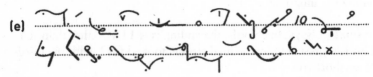

PHRASING

We've already seen examples of phrases in which a word is
omitted from outlines, and we can do this where there is no risk of
misreading. Here are some more:

1 *Omitting the word* a

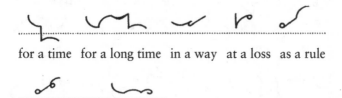

for a time   for a long time   in a way   at a loss   as a rule

as a result   for a moment

2 *Omitting the word* and

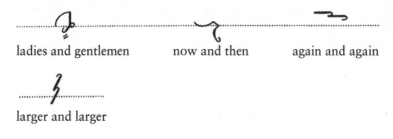

ladies and gentlemen   now and then   again and again

larger and larger

3 *Repetition of the comparative form of adjectives. Here we
omit everything except the first stroke of the first adjective:*

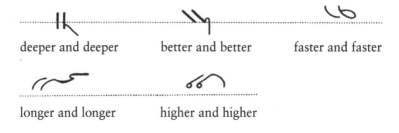

deeper and deeper   better and better   faster and faster

longer and longer   higher and higher

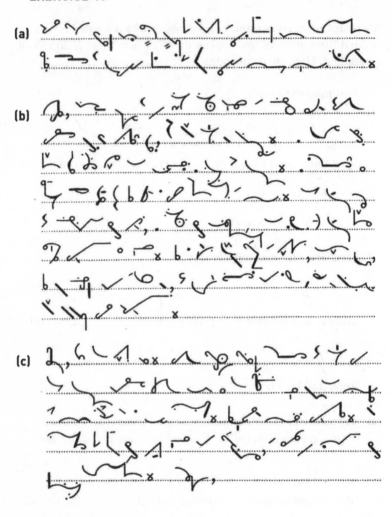

(a)

(b)

(c)

Compound consonants

Consonants are often pronounced as a group of two or three or even four as in words like <u>cl</u>ub (2), <u>str</u>aight (3) and twe<u>lfths</u> (4).

When these clusters appear at the beginning of a syllable, then they are called **compound consonants**. The two initial hooks L and R are compound consonants, though it is more practical to call them initial hooks because they can be used both as syllables and as consonants.

> We have three other such compounds used initially in syllables – KW, GW and WH. They are written by adding a large hook to the K, G and W strokes: ⌒ ⌒ ✓

KW begins with a hook written left motion (anticlockwise) just like an L hook but twice the size. Do not allow the writing of a large hook to edge you into writing a longer stroke for K – keep it the normal length.

GW is exactly the same as KW, but with a heavier stroke:

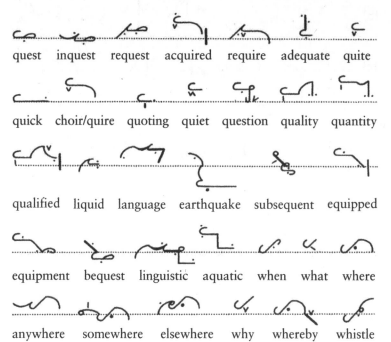

quest   inquest   request   acquired   require   adequate   quite

quick   choir/quire   quoting   quiet   question   quality   quantity

qualified   liquid   language   earthquake   subsequent   equipped

equipment   bequest   linguistic   aquatic   when   what   where

anywhere   somewhere   elsewhere   why   whereby   whistle

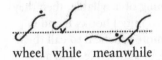

wheel   while   meanwhile

W and WH

Some people who speak English make no difference between
a W and a WH sound. They pronounce *where* in exactly the
same way as *wear*. In shorthand the distinction is always made.

EXERCISE 42

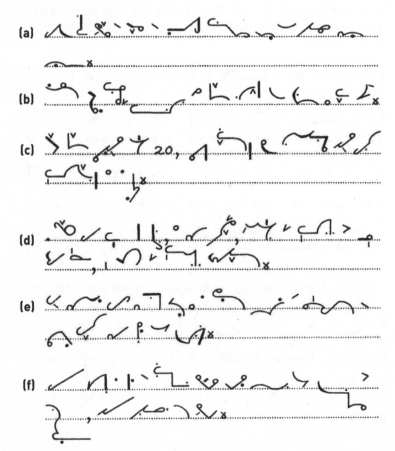

(a)

(b)

(c) 20,

(d)

(e)

(f)

SHORT FORMS

knowledge   acknowledge   acknowledging   acknowledged

acknowledgment   together   altogether

Intersections

1 *A stroke N may be intersected to represent* enquire, enquiry *or* enquired. *Add a dot to this for* enquiring *or a circle for* enquiries.

may we enquire   your enquiry   we have enquired   we are enquiring

our enquiries   enquiry bureau

2 *An R upward may be intersected to represent* require, requirement, *or* required. *Add a dot to make* requiring, *or a circle S for* requirements

we shall require   your requirements   we were required

we shall be requiring   our requirements

Phrasing

More phrases showing the omission of a word are:

by: 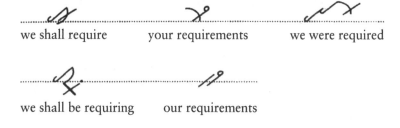 *side by side* *year by year* have: ...._ *would have been* ......_ *must have been*

in: ...._ *stock in trade* ......_ *bear in mind*

of: ....._ *point of view* ....._ *first of all*

EXERCISE 43

(a)

(b)

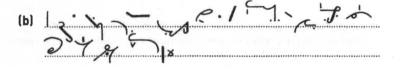

(c)

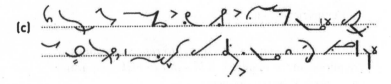

(d)

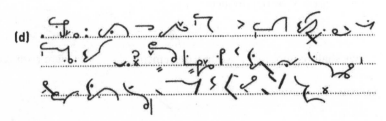

(e)

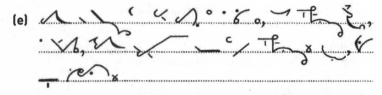

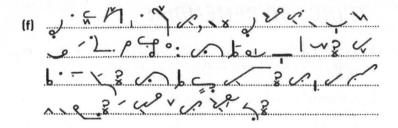

(f)

EXERCISE 44

Write in shorthand, afterwards checking with the key (phrasing is indicated by hyphens):

Dear-Miss Clark,

Thank-you for-your-request for extra supplies of art paper for-your branch. We-are-able-to obtain only a few quires a month and-the demand is always much greater-than-the supply. We-will increase-the quantity allo-cated to-your branch in April when we-hope to-have an extra source of supplies. Thank-you also for-the returns for last-month and-we-are-glad to see what progress you-are making in sales in an area where progress is-not easy. The receipts to-gether-with our cheque for expenses are enclosed. Let-us-know as-soon-as you-are-able-to appoint the new sales assistant required in-the branch.

Yours-sincerely,

Dictation time

This exercise is included in the dictations on the audio.
Try Ex 44.A now, then to help fix your earlier learning,
try Ex 38.B.

THINGS TO REMEMBER

▶ *The -MENT suffix can be written with M hooked for N or by stroke N – either way it is then halved for T.*

▶ *L is written downwards after stroke N.*

▶ *If a -MENT suffix is written as N halved, downward L can be added to make -MENTAL. If -MENT is written as a M hooked for N, then M, N, T L must be written in full.*

▶ *The -LY suffix can be disjoined if necessary.*

▶ *A large hook can be added to K, G or H strokes to show KW, GW or WH.*

11

L and R hooks with curves

In this unit you will learn:
* *about adding L and R hooks to curved strokes*
* *about circles and hooks*
* *when not to hook*
* *the rules for L and R in stressed words*
* *how hooks can be reversed*

Initial hooks to curved strokes

The initial hooks L and R can be added to curved strokes just as they can be to straight strokes. As they are always written *inside* curves, to distinguish the two, the R hook is written small and the L hook is written large.

R hooks:

FR   VR   ThR   THR   SHR   ZHR   MR   NR

L hooks:

FL   VL   ThL   SHL   ML   NL

Notes:

Both the voiced and unvoiced forms of TH have R hooks.

Neither the voiced sounds THL nor ZHL occur in normal English words, so there are no hooked forms for these sounds.

As with hooks to straight strokes, some of these can be used either as consonants, as in *frame* ![frame symbol] or *flame* ![flame symbol] or as syllables, as in *differ* ![differ symbol] or *shuffle* ![shuffle symbol].

These can also be used as syllables:

VR THR ZHR MR NR THL SHL ML NL

Examples of hooked curves as consonants

free Friday thread throb shrub shrink flow Vladivostok

flood athletic flexible flying frequent afraid fragile fruit

freight throwing frame flame

Examples of their use as syllables:

offer diver measure leisure rumour climber owner

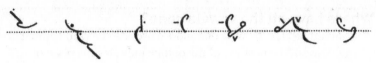

banner   favourable   tether   other   otherwise   survivor   fresher

energy   honourable   mineral   funeral   powerful   faithful

joyful   devil   partial   camel   penalty   enamel   animal

signalling   social

The N-R-L sequence

Notice how the downward L is used after N hooked for R in
mineral _____ and *funeral* _____. Downward L is also

used after N, N halved and -ING.

Writing notes

When writing the initial hooks to curved strokes:

(a) *Keep the hooks round.*

(b) *Keep the R hook small.*

(c) *L hook must be noticeably larger, so it is not confused with the R hook.*

(d) *Do not let the size of the L hook induce you to increase the size of the stroke to which the hook is written.*

(e) *Keep the shape of the stroke correct.*

Finally, remember that writing lightly is vital for writing quickly. There are no heavy strokes in shorthand – only light strokes and still lighter strokes.

Where have all the vowels gone?

It should be clear by now that most words can be read without any vowels. The position of the outline indicates the place of the first, and often the strokes themselves indicate whether a vowel precedes or follows. However, even the most skilled and experienced writers never throw out all the vowels. There are many times when the inclusion of one vital vowel will make reading back instant and unambiguous. For example, an initial vowel not otherwise indicated is most helpful in transcribing, and so too are diphones and diphthongs.

Which vowels to omit and which to retain is a matter of experience and of personal preference. Note the practice followed in all the subsequent shorthand material.

Vowels will be largely omitted in exercises from this point on, though they will continue to be written in words used to illustrate new theory when they first appear.

EXERCISE 45

(e)

CIRCLES TO INITIAL HOOKS TO CURVED STROKES

The circle S may be tucked inside either an R hook or an L hook to a curved stroke and used in the middle of words, as in:

suffer   decipher   sooner   summer   savoury   gossamer   civil

Savell   civilly

Note also how final vowels may be added after a curved stroke initially hooked.

WHEN NOT TO HOOK

In one-syllable words consisting mainly of a consonant and a vowel plus R or L, the hook is not used:

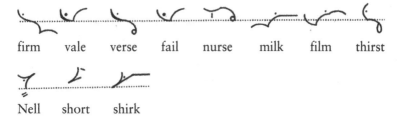

firm   vale   verse   fail   nurse   milk   film   thirst

Nell   short   shirk

If the hooks are not used in the root word, then they are not used in the derivatives either. In this way families of words can have similar basic outlines and are thus easier to read and to write. You can see this in the following which are all derived from the last set of examples:

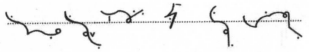

firmness versify nursery shortage thirsty filmstrip

In words that have a consonant and a diphthong (or a diphone or a triphone) plus R or L, the hooked form is not used, for example.

senior junior healthier manual menial casual

Stress rules with R and L hooks

The rules about stress in relation to strokes initially hooked for R and L are the same for curves as they are for straight strokes. As it is important to know when initially hooked curves may be used and when they may not, the rule is explained again here. This time initially hooked curves will serve as our examples.

All English words of more than one syllable have one that is strongly stressed. For example in the _caramel_ the stress falls on the first; in _invention_ on the second, and in _entertain_ on the third syllable.

In any word formed from a consonant plus a vowel plus R or L, we can use the initial hook or separate strokes – consonant and R or consonant and L.

The rule is that if this combination occurs in an unstressed syllable, then we use the initially hooked form regardless of what vowel is between them (unless it is a diphthong, diphone or triphone – see above).

For example, in *forestall* the FORE- syllable is unstressed so we can use the hooked form and write it, without the vowel, like this:

Similarly, in *volcano* the VOL- syllable is unstressed so we can use the hooked form. Again, the vowel between V and L is not written in, but it does decide the place of the outline on the line.

Here are some words where unstressed syllables with curve stroke consonant + vowel + R or L are written with the hooked form:

forget   advertise   foretell   philosopher   fulfil   privilege

chivalry shellac calomel average verbose

If the hooked form is used in a root word it is retained in derivatives even though, as sometimes happens, the stress shifts, as in:

advertise advertisement philosophy philosophic

civil civilised civility

If the hooked form is **not** used in a root word, then it is not used in derivatives either, even though the stress may shift, as in:

fertile fertility moral morality shell eggshell

EXERCISE 46

(a)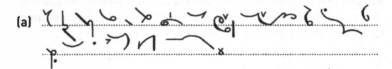

(b)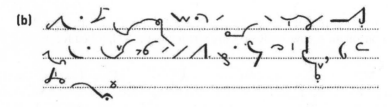

(c)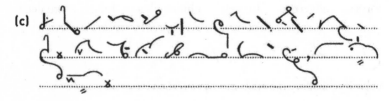

(d)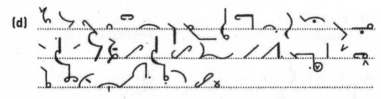

(e)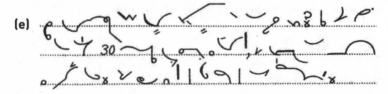

(f)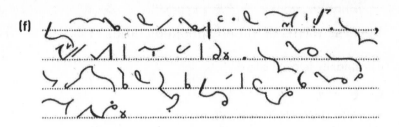

(g)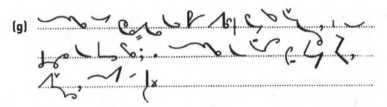

Reverse forms of initially hooked curves

The initially hooked curves

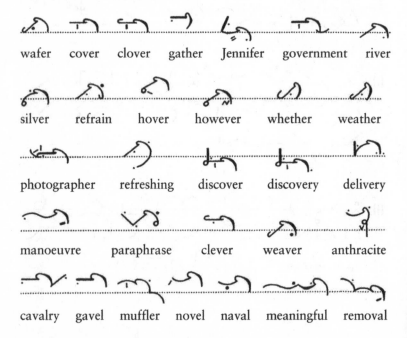

FR   VR   ThR   THR   FL   VL

have reverse forms. These are written with a clockwise motion and appear as:

FR   VR   ThR   THR   FL   VL

These reverse forms are always used after all horizontals and all upstrokes, whether straight or curved. Why? Because it is not possible to write the ordinary forms of the initially hooked curves after horizontals or upstrokes:

wafer   cover   clover   gather   Jennifer   government   river

silver   refrain   hover   however   whether   weather

photographer   refreshing   discover   discovery   delivery

manoeuvre   paraphrase   clever   weaver   anthracite

cavalry   gavel   muffler   novel   naval   meaningful   removal

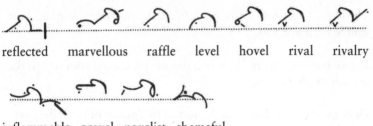

reflected   marvellous   raffle   level   hovel   rival   rivalry

inflammable   gravel   novelist   shameful

If an R appears in the spelling of a word, it is always shown
in shorthand even though it may not seem to be pronounced.
For example:

fought   fort

The reasons for this are:

(a) *The inclusion of the R always makes reading easier and helps to
distinguish words that might otherwise have identical outlines.*
(b) *The presence of an R often has a modifying effect on the
vowel or diphthong that precedes it.*
(c) *In some forms of spoken English (as, for example, in Scotland)
the R is sounded more than in other forms.*

SHORT FORMS

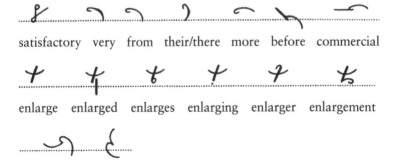

satisfactory   very   from   their/there   more   before   commercial

enlarge   enlarged   enlarges   enlarging   enlarger   enlargement

influential   thankful

The important short forms *very*, *from*, *their/there* are formed from simple reverse forms.

Before is a short form because a reverse FR is used contrary to the rule given above.

Once you learn *enlarge*, all the rest of this group of six follow on naturally.

In writing *influential*, ensure that the reverse form FL comes through the line.

EXERCISE 47

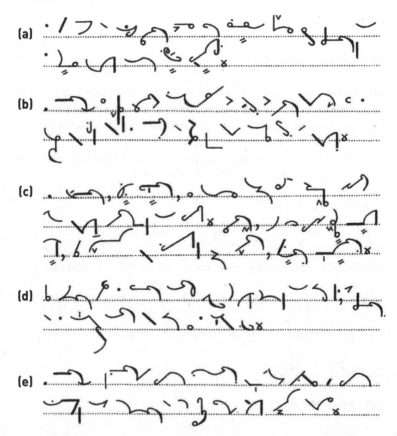

(a)

(b)

(c)

(d)

(e)

Phrasing

There are lots of phrases this time, but they are all important to know as they occur frequently. Take the time to learn them well.

1 Than *phrases. The N hook used for* than *in phrases is added to initially curved strokes, as in:*

more than   sooner than   finer than

2 *Initially hooked strokes are used in phrasing like this:*

our: .... in .... in our .... in our own .... in our interests

far: .... far .... so far .... very far .... too far
.... how far

appear: .... appear .... it appears .... which appear
.... it may appear

part: ....part .... your part .... some parts
.... in all parts of the world

course: .... course .... of course .... in due course
.... in the course of

time: .... time .... sometime .... at all times
.... at the same time

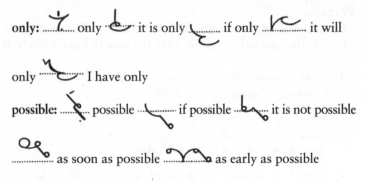

only: ⋯⋯⋯ only ⋯⋯⋯ it is only ⋯⋯⋯ if only ⋯⋯⋯ it will

only ⋯⋯⋯ I have only

possible: ⋯⋯⋯ possible ⋯⋯⋯ if possible ⋯⋯⋯ it is not possible

⋯⋯⋯ as soon as possible ⋯⋯⋯ as early as possible

3 *Omitting T from the ST loop:*

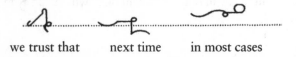

we trust that   next time   in most cases

4 *There phrases:*

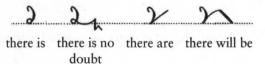

there is   there is no   there are   there will be
            doubt

Intersections
A TH may be intersected, or joined if it is more convenient,
to represent *month*:

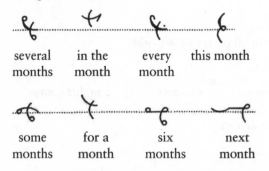

several   in the   every   this month
months   month   month

some   for a   six   next
months   month   months   month

(a)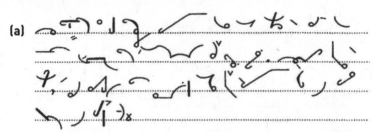

(b)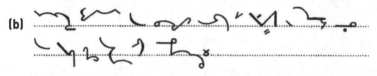

(c)

(d)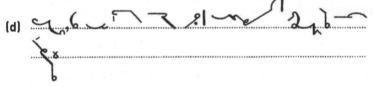

(e)

(f)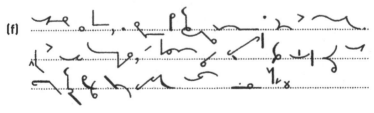

(g)

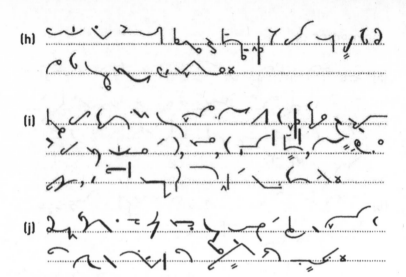

(h)

(i)

(j)

EXERCISE 49

Write in shorthand, afterwards checking from the key (phrasing is indicated by hyphens):

Jennifer went down to-the meadows near-the river bank to gather wild flowers. At-the-time she set out the weather was sunny, but sultry and stifling. She went two-miles along-the towpath in her search for a variety of wild flowers as-far-as-the old bridge at Liversedge. It-was there that-the great storm broke. What began as a refreshing shower very quickly became a downpour of more-than tropical violence with hailstones as-large-as walnuts and ceaseless lightning of dazzling brilliance. Jennifer took refuge from-the hailstones beneath an arch of-the bridge. But such was-the quantity of-water that fell, that-the river soon became a torrent, and she was obliged to-seek help from-the Glover family. They lived in a large grange close by-the bridge at Liversedge. It-was this chance meeting that began-the famous romance which this novel tells.

Dictation time
This exercise is included in the dictations on the audio. Try Ex 49.A now. To help fix your earlier learning, try Ex 44.B.

Review

Read, copy, and then re-read from your own copy each of the four passages that follow. Then re-transcribe them back into shorthand from the key without reference to your original shorthand. Check the result.

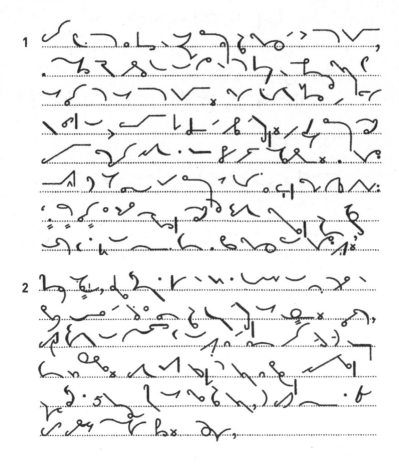

3

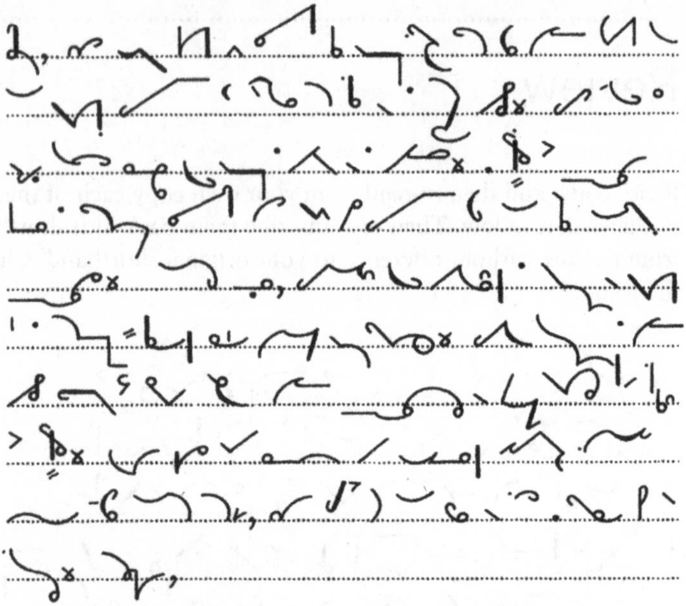

4

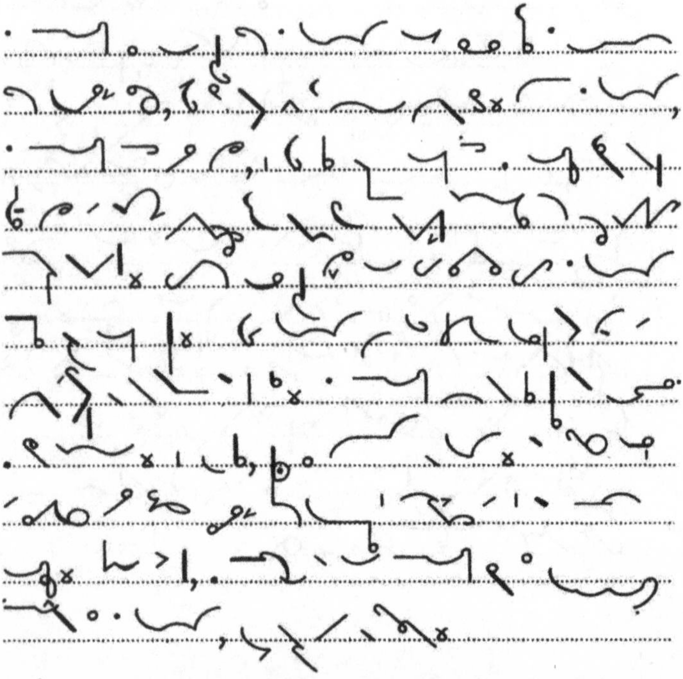

THINGS TO REMEMBER

▶ *The L and R hooks can be added to curved strokes. They are always written inside the curve – make the L hook Large.*

▶ *Circle S can be tucked inside a hook.*

▶ *Don't use L and R hooks in one syllable words.*

▶ *L and R hooks can be used for the unstressed syllables.*

▶ *Hooks can be reversed where necessary.*

12

More hooks

In this unit you will learn:
- *about the suffix -SHUN*
- *about the F/V hook*

-SHUN hook

The suffix -SHUN, pronounced sometimes with unvoiced SH and sometimes with voiced ZH, is very common in English. It is variously spelled, e.g.: *fashion, relation, Persian, invasion*, but of course it is the sound that is represented in shorthand and not the spelling.

Note that in the first two examples, *fashion and relation*, -SHUN is pronounced with the unvoiced SH and in the last two, *Persian* and *invasion*, with voiced ZH.

-SHUN HOOK TO CURVES

-SHUN is written as a large hook inside a curved stroke, and at the end of the stroke. Circle S may be added:

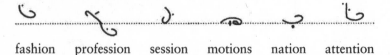

| fashion | profession | session | motions | nation | attention |

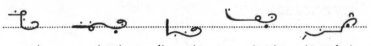

extension examinations dimensions vaccination inoculation

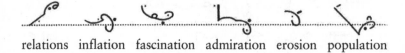

relations inflation fascination admiration erosion population

A third-place dot vowel before a -SHUN hook to any curved stroke is written inside the hook. All other third-place vowels, diphthongs, triphones or diphones are written outside the hook in the third place:

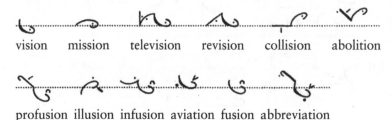

vision mission television revision collision abolition

profusion illusion infusion aviation fusion abbreviation

Although -SHUN is always written at the end of a stroke, it is often found n the middle of words, as in:

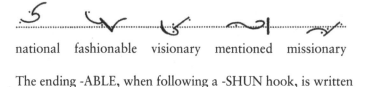

national fashionable visionary mentioned missionary

The ending -ABLE, when following a -SHUN hook, is written

with ⌄ or ⌇ disjoined and written close to the -SHUN hook, as:

unfashionable   tensionable   mentionable

EXERCISE 50

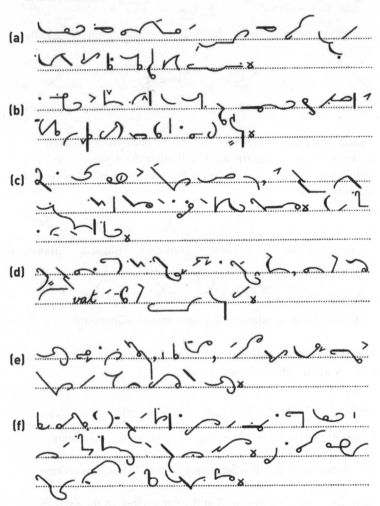

(a)

(b)

(c)

(d)

(e)

(f)

SHUN TO STRAIGHT STROKES

When -SHUN follows a straight stroke, it is obvious that it may be
written either on one side of the stroke or on the other, as in:

K-SHUN   K-SHUN

There are rules to govern which side of a straight stroke to write the -SHUN. They are given here in order of priority.

(a) **If the straight stroke has an initial hook or an initial circle,** *then the -SHUN is always written on the side opposite to that initial attachment. The reason for the rule is to make writing easier by keeping the straight stroke straight:*

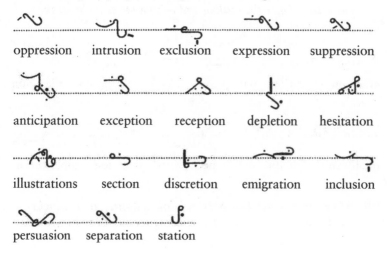

| oppression | intrusion | exclusion | expression | suppression |

| anticipation | exception | reception | depletion | hesitation |

| illustrations | section | discretion | emigration | inclusion |

| persuasion | separation | station |

Exceptions to the rule!

For *stationary/stationery* and *exceptional*, the -SHUN hook is written on the same side as the initial attachment to enable the derivative word to be written from the root.

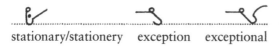

stationary/stationery   exception   exceptional

(b) **On the right side of simple T,D or J.** *The idea is to keep the hand moving forward along the line of writing:*

tuition   invitation   optician   imitation   plantation   magician

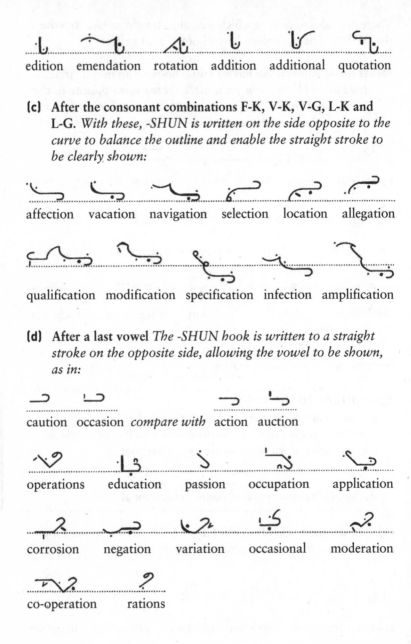

edition   emendation   rotation   addition   additional   quotation

(c) **After the consonant combinations F-K, V-K, V-G, L-K and L-G.** *With these, -SHUN is written on the side opposite to the curve to balance the outline and enable the straight stroke to be clearly shown:*

affection   vacation   navigation   selection   location   allegation

qualification   modification   specification   infection   amplification

(d) **After a last vowel** *The -SHUN hook is written to a straight stroke on the opposite side, allowing the vowel to be shown, as in:*

caution   occasion   *compare with*   action   auction

operations   education   passion   occupation   application

corrosion   negation   variation   occasional   moderation

co-operation   rations

(e) **After a consonant.** *When the form of the word is consonant plus -SHUN with no vowel in between, write the -SHUN on whichever the side of the straight stroke will not imply a vowel. For example, in the sequence P…R, a vowel after the R would be written below and to the right of its stroke. Hence, with* portion ╲╱ *the -SHUN is written clockwise, implying no vowel, but in* operation ╲╱ *it is written anticlockwise, to indicate a vowel after the R.*

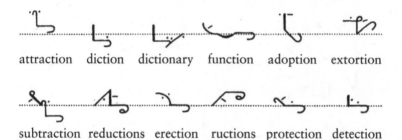

attraction diction dictionary function adoption extortion

subtraction reductions erection ructions protection detection

(f) **-SHUN is followed by a vowel and ST.** *In this combination the -SHUN hook is not possible, so SH or ZH + stroke N + ST is used, as in:*

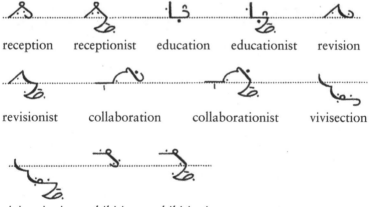

reception receptionist education educationist revision

revisionist collaboration collaborationist vivisection

vivisectionist exhibition exhibitionist

EXERCISE 51

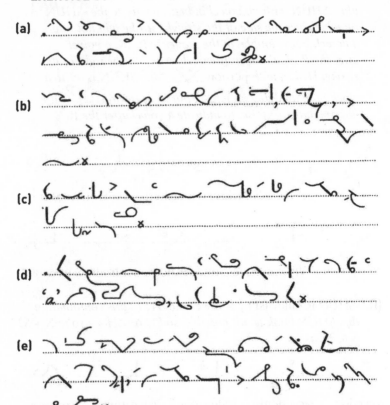

(a)

(b)

(c)

(d)

(e)

CIRCLE S/Z FOLLOWED BY -SHUN

There are a number of common words in which the combination S (or NS) + vowel + -SHUN occurs. To write these, the circle is carried through the stroke to which it is attached so as to form a small hook. Circle S may be added to this.

In this combination, the vowel is never a stroke vowel and never a first-place vowel, so we have only to distinguish third-place and second-place vowels. This is done by writing in the third-place dot vowels as shown and indicating the second-place vowels by omitting them altogether. In most contexts such distinction is rarely necessary, for example:

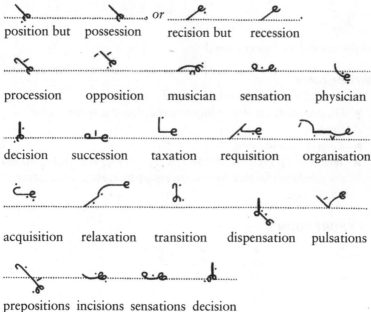

position but   possession   *or*   recision but   recession

procession   opposition   musician   sensation   physician

decision   succession   taxation   requisition   organisation

acquisition   relaxation   transition   dispensation   pulsations

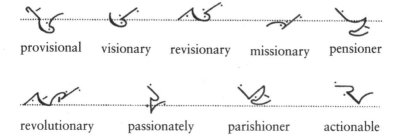

prepositions incisions sensations decision

Other derivatives

S (or NS) + vowel + SHUN followed by L has to be written with a disjoined L close up to the root outline. Some other derivatives from roots having final -SHUN can be written joined. Others have to be written differently or disjoined:

provisional   visionary   revisionary   missionary   pensioner

revolutionary   passionately   parishioner   actionable

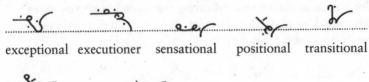

exceptional   executioner   sensational   positional   transitional

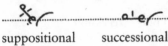

suppositional   successional

Writing notes
- ▶ *Write the -SHUN hook large and round.*
- ▶ *Do not allow its size to increase the size of standard length strokes.*
- ▶ *Keep the hook open.*
- ▶ *Write the S/SHUN or NS/SHUN by carrying the circle through the stroke no farther than is necessary to make a small, neat, open hook.*

SHORT FORMS

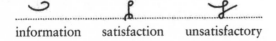

information   satisfaction   unsatisfactory

Note how each of these short forms is made by omitting a whole syllable, yet leaving a readable framework which clearly suggests the word.

Intersections
1 *A KR hook may be intersected for* corporation, *as in:*

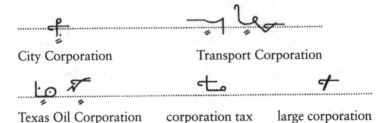

City Corporation   Transport Corporation

Texas Oil Corporation   corporation tax   large corporation

2 *A T may be intersected for* attention, *as in:*

prompt attention	to our attention	my attention	immediate attention

EXERCISE 52

(a)
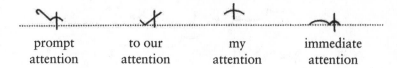

(b)
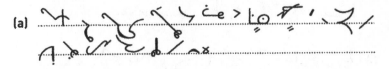

(c)
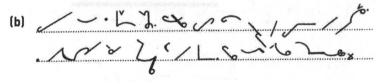

(d)
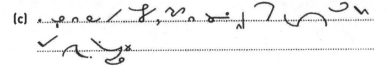

(e)

(f)
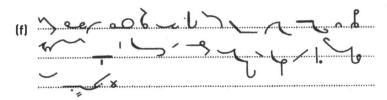

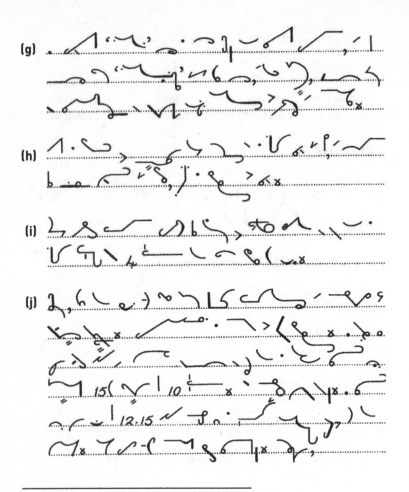

F/V hook

In addition to initial hooks R and L, and the final hook N, there is also a similar small round hook that represents the sounds F or V. It is written only to straight strokes as shown. Circle S/Z may be added:

tough   dive   beef   chief   wife   rough   cave   proof   approve

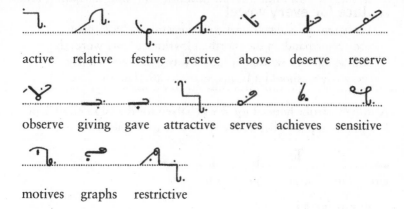

active relative festive restive above deserve reserve

observe giving gave attractive serves achieves sensitive

motives graphs restrictive

Writing note

Hook F/V is written to straight strokes only, and is (i) small,
(ii) round and (iii) anticlockwise. When the circle S/Z is tucked
inside the hook, it takes an oval rather than a circular form, and
this is acceptable.

In a word ending with F or V plus vowel, then the stroke must be
used. This is a further instance of the fact that the way in which an
outline is written often indicates the presence or absence of vowels:

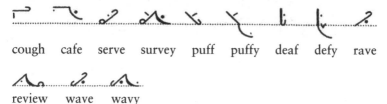

cough cafe serve survey puff puffy deaf defy rave

review wave wavy

The same is true of words that end in F or V plus any vowel(s) plus
S/Z. They, too, must be written with stroke and circle:

grievous advise refuse previous surface mischievous

A place for every vowel

These two rules illustrate a more general rule of Pitman 2000 Shorthand: in the shorthand writing of any word, the outline must be written in such a way that there is a place for every vowel, should it be necessary to insert all the vowels.

A straight stroke hooked for F/V is halved for the addition of T or D and this applies whether the word is a monosyllable or not:

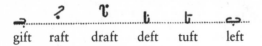

gift   raft   draft   deft   tuft   left

EXERCISE 53

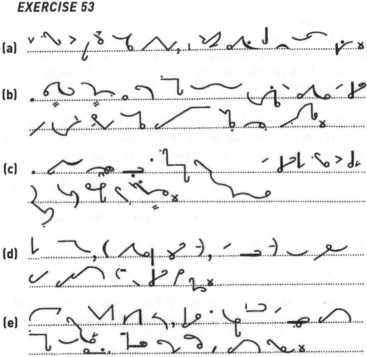

The hook F/V may also be used in the middle of words between certain strokes.

(a) *between two straight downstrokes, as in:*

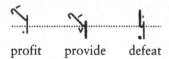

profit   provide   defeat

(b) *between a straight downstroke and strokes Th, S, Z, K, G or N, as in:*

diphthong privacy proviso traffic defect defence juvenile

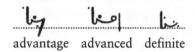

advantage advanced definite

(c) *between two straight horizontal strokes, as in:*

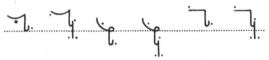

biographic   photographic   orthographic   stenographic

If a root word is written with an F/V hook at the end, derived or compound words retain this hook, as in:

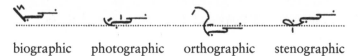

native nativity festive festivity active activity

Short forms

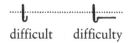

difficult   difficulty

1 *The F/V hook is used in phrases, in particular for* of *which very frequently follows nouns, as in:*

out   out of   rate of   rate of interest   state of   state of affairs   part of

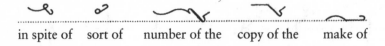

in spite of   sort of   number of the   copy of the   make of

It is impossible to list here all such phrases because the opportunities of adding the F/V hook for *of* and a further tick for *the* are continually arising. It is clearly a saving in time to write a phrase like *group of the* with an added hook and tick, rather than with a separate *of the* shortform. The latter is not wrong, but the former is preferable. Here's *group of the* written both ways:

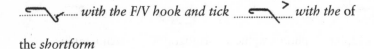

with the F/V hook and tick *with the* of

the *shortform*

2 *The F/V hook is also used for:*
(a) have, *as in:*

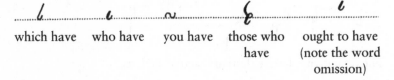

which have   who have   you have   those who   ought to have
                                    have   (note the word
                                                  omission)

But not in:

we have   we have been

(b) off, *as in:*

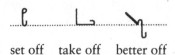

set off   take off   better off

(c) *Note the use of the F/V hook in these phrases:*

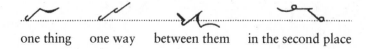

at all   at all events   such events   which events

In some common phrases, the N hook may be omitted:

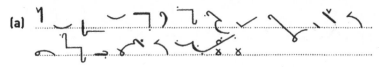

one thing   one way   between them   in the second place

EXERCISE 54

(a)

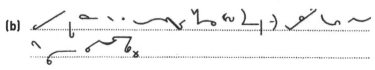

(b)

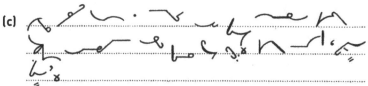

(c)

(d)

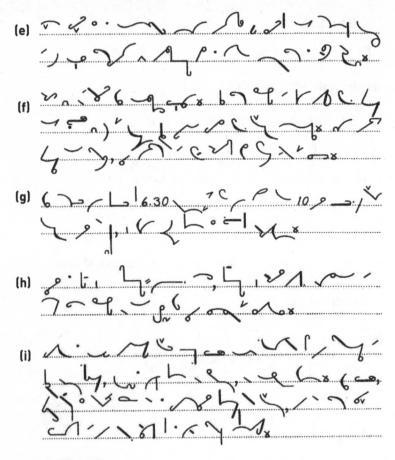

(e)

(f)

(g)

(h)

(i)

EXERCISE 55

Write in shorthand, afterwards checking from the key (phrasing is indicated by hyphens):

The cafe at-the top-of-the hill called Kate's Cook-In is well worth a visit as-those-who-have-been will tell-you. They serve you with very-good meals at low-prices and in-your-present state-of lack-of money, you-have good reasons for spending as little as-possible. At-all-events, you-will-be better-off taking one hot meal a day there than eating the poor fare that-they serve up in-your guest house. This-is a copy of-the menu at-the cafe for Tuesday of-last week.

Dictation time

This exercise is included in the dictations on the audio.
Try Ex 55.A now, then come back later and try Ex 55.B.

THINGS TO REMEMBER

▶ A -SHUN ending can be shown by a large hook added at the end of a stroke.

▶ The -SHUN hook is written inside a curved stroke. With straight strokes it goes on the side which produces the best outline – study the rules carefully.

▶ The F/V hook can only be added to straight strokes. It must be distinctively smaller than a -SHUN hook.

13

....

Speed strokes

In this unit you will learn:
- *how doubling a stroke can add a syllable*
- *shortcuts for CON, COM and similar sounds*

Some sounds are so common in English that Pitman 2000 shorthand has special strokes to replace complete syllables. We've met several of these on the way through the book. In this unit we will look at the techniques for representing two sets of very common combinations.

_____

Doubling

Writing a stroke twice its normal length adds to it the syllable -TER or

-DER or -THER or (in common words) -TURE.

DOUBLING CURVES

Any curved stroke may be doubled in length to add these final syllables, as in:

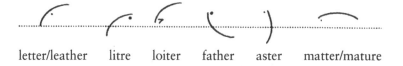

letter/leather   litre   loiter   father   aster   matter/mature

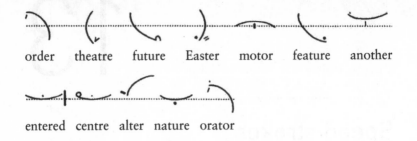

order theatre future Easter motor feature another

entered centre alter nature orator

Writing notes

1 *Write a double-length stroke with a free cursive movement, and make it at least twice as long as normal – the exact length does not matter.*

As with the other shorthand principles that require something large – like SES, STER, SHUN, KW, GW, WH, or the L hook to curves – this may be written in a slightly exaggerated form, but only if that does not affect the size of the connected or adjacent strokes.

2 *All the downward curves are bound to come through the line. Strokes M, N and upward L may take their correct positions according to the first vowel in the words.*

This doubling of curved strokes may be used in the middle of an outline, as you can see in some of these:

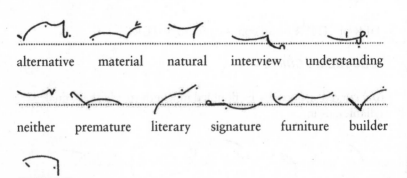

alternative material natural interview understanding

neither premature literary signature furniture builder

moderate

Curved strokes with an initial hook R or L or a final N hook may be doubled, as in:

flutter inventor reminder calendar shredder founders

In a small group of words, curved strokes may be doubled for the addition of the sound -TEER, however spelled, as in:

austere frontier volunteer muleteer arterial

EXERCISE 56

(a)

(b)

(c)

(d)

(e)

DOUBLING STRAIGHT STROKES

Straight strokes may be doubled in length to add -TER, -DER, -THER or -TURE, but only when they follow another stroke, or are finally hooked for N or F/V, as in:

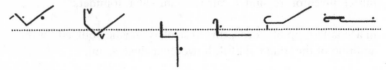

operator typewriter dictator director quarter agriculture

picture porter protector tractor structure indicator painter

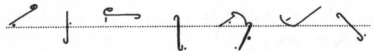

rafters tender squander drifter refrigerator further printer

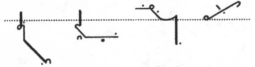

distributor duplicator expenditure surrender

WHEN NOT TO DOUBLE

Do not use doubling in outlines with two strokes of unequal length and no angle between them (which would have made them more readable), e.g.:

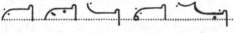

elector locator factor selector navigator

Do not double straight strokes in the middle of an outline.
It would not be obvious whether two identical strokes followed
one another (as in *cook* or *cake*) or whether doubling was being
used. So we write:

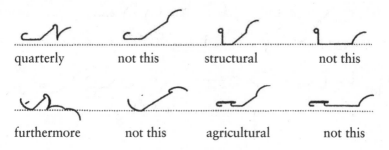

quarterly   not this   structural   not this

furthermore   not this   agricultural   not this

Do not double if a final vowel follows the syllables -TER, etc. e.g.:

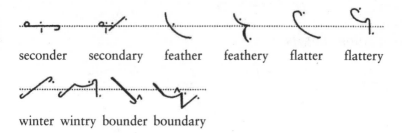

seconder   secondary   feather   feathery   flatter   flattery

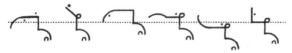

winter wintry bounder boundary

Sometimes, if the final syllable -TURE cannot be represented by
doubling, then it is written with T and R down, as in:

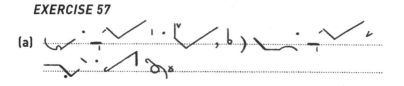

ligature pasture lecture mixture fixture texture

EXERCISE 57

(a)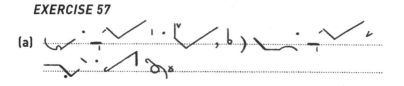

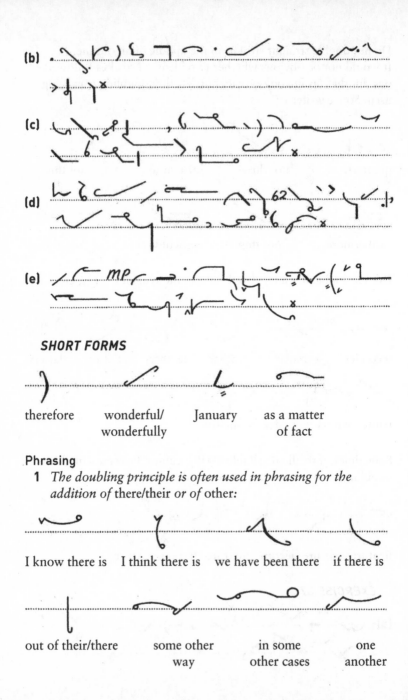

(b)

(c)

(d)

(e)

SHORT FORMS

| therefore | wonderful/ wonderfully | January | as a matter of fact |

Phrasing

1 *The doubling principle is often used in phrasing for the addition of* there/their *or of* other:

| I know there is | I think there is | we have been there | if there is |

| out of their/there | some other way | in some other cases | one another |

2 *Doubling is also used for* dear *and* order:

my dear sir   very dear   in order   in order that

But note this short form for a very common phrase *in order to*: ....

3 *Omission of* of the:

out of the question   one of the most   in all parts of the world

freedom of the press

4 *Omission of* the:

on the subject of   in the   for the   all over the world
                      event of   sake of

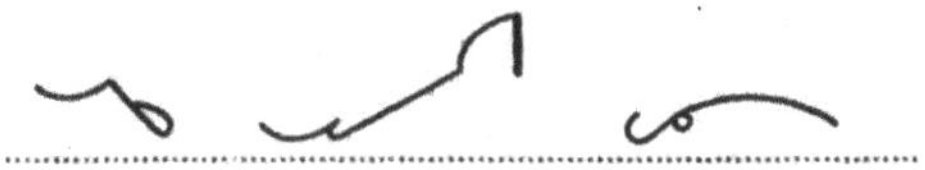

in the past   in the world   what is
                               the matter

EXERCISE 58

(a)

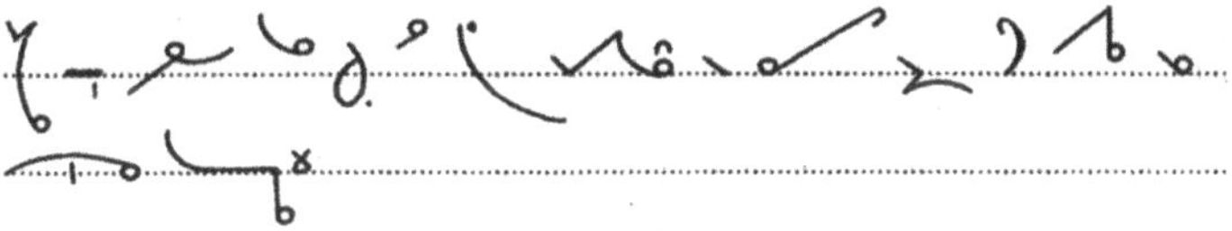

(b)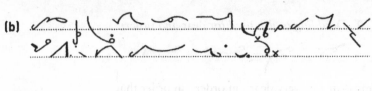

(c)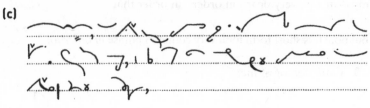

(d)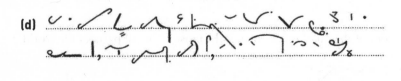

(e)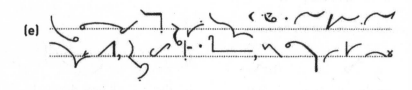

(f)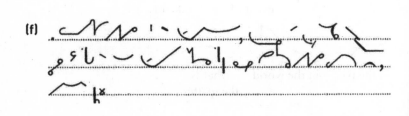

(g)

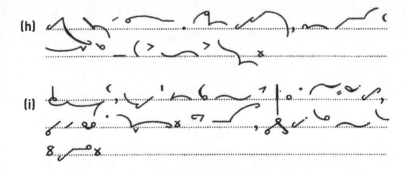

(h)

(i)

CON- or COM-

PREFIX CON- OR COM-

In the Concise Oxford Dictionary (1982) there are twenty-two pages of words that begin with CON- or COM-, totalling nearly five hundred words, most of them common ones.

Shorthand represents this initial prefix with a dot placed just before the first stroke in the outline begins. The position of the outline is fixed by the vowel place of the first vowel after the CON- or COM-:

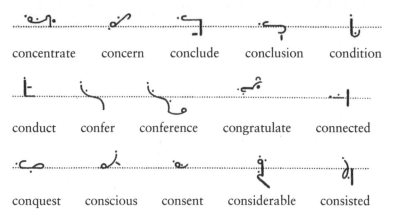

| concentrate | concern | conclude | conclusion | condition |

| conduct | confer | conference | congratulate | connected |

| conquest | conscious | consent | considerable | consisted |

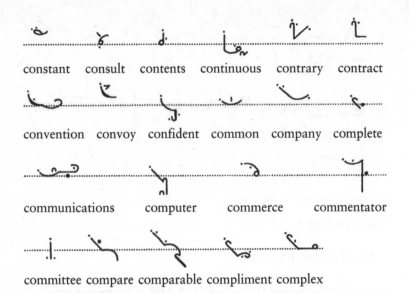

constant   consult   contents   continuous   contrary   contract

convention   convoy   confident   common   company   complete

communications   computer   commerce   commentator

committee   compare   comparable   compliment   complex

A second way of writing initial CON- or COM- is to write the outline for the word that begins with CON- or COM- close up to the one that precedes it:

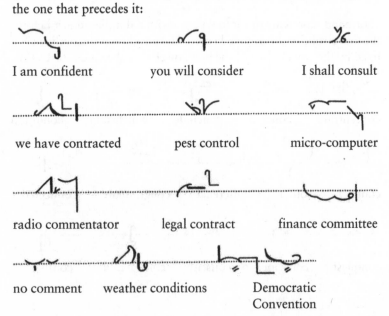

I am confident   you will consider   I shall consult

we have contracted   pest control   micro-computer

radio commentator   legal contract   finance committee

no comment   weather conditions   Democratic Convention

MEDIAL -CON-, -COM-, -COG-, -CUM-

When a word has the syllable -CON-, or -COM, or -COG-, or -CUM- in the middle, it is written by disjoining the stroke or strokes following the syllable, but writing them close up. For example, *subconscious* is formed from *sub* and *scious* like this:

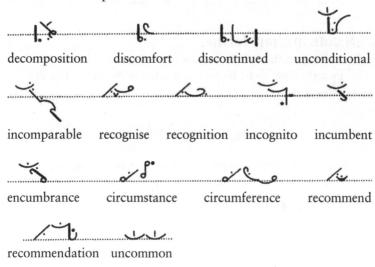

sub   scious   subconscious

Some more examples:

decomposition   discomfort   discontinued   unconditional

incomparable   recognise   recognition   incognito   incumbent

encumbrance   circumstance   circumference   recommend

recommendation   uncommon

EXERCISE 59

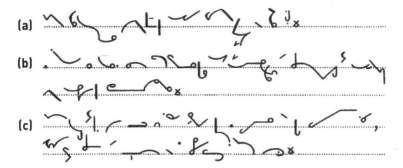

(a)

(b)

(c)

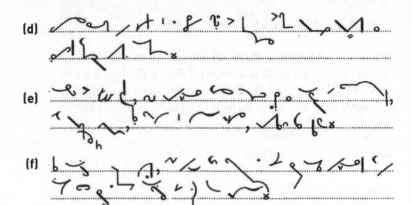

(d)

(e)

(f)

CON dots in short forms

You can omit the CON- dot when writing a word close up to an upward dash short form, but not single downward or dot short forms:

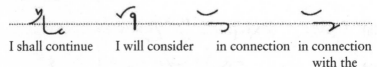

and contact the   on the computer   all committees   of the committee

---

SHORT FORMS

nevertheless   notwithstanding

Phrasing

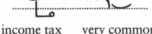

I shall continue   I will consider   in connection   in connection with the

income tax   very common

(a)

(b)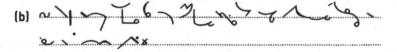

(c)

(d)

(e)

(f)

(g)

(h)

THINGS TO REMEMBER

▶ *Writing a stroke double its normal length adds -TER, -THER and similar endings.*

▶ *Doubling cannot be used where it may cause confusion.*

▶ *A dot before the first stroke is a shortcut for* CON *or* COM.

▶ CON, COM, COG *and* CUM *in the middle of words can be omitted and indicated by disjoining the syllables before and after.*

14

....

Last words

Figures

In this unit you will learn:
- *how to write figures*
- *how to write negative forms of words*
- *about the -SHIP suffix*
- *when to insert vowels*

Apart from o and 8, it is normal practice to use shorthand for

figures up to ten and for round numbers like ....(30) or

..........(90). This is not a hard and fast rule. For example, it is quite common to use numbers in dates:

4th August   2nd January

N may be used for *hundred*, Th for *thousand*, M for *million* and B for *billion*, set out like this:

..........= seven hundred ....= five thousand

..........= twenty-three million ....= seven hundred thousand

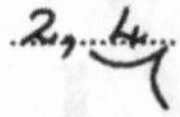

2, 4 or *2 4* = two million, four hundred thousand

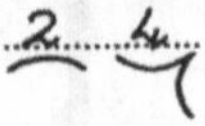

3 4 = three billion, four hundred million

The pound can be added to show sums of money. Note its position:

3 = £3,000, *242* = £242,000,000 *7 22* = £7.22

Anything other than round numbers are normally written out in figures:

17,222 = £17,222 *437,260* = 437,260 *tons*

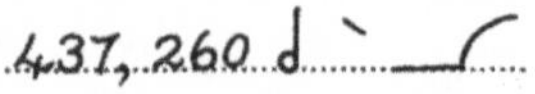

of coal

The 24-hour clock may be written as shown:

18 9 = 1800 hours *2352 9* = 2352 hours

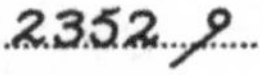

Normal time references to am and pm are as shown:

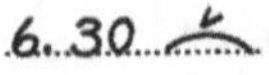

6.30 = 6.30 am *4* = 4 pm

EXERCISE 61

(a) 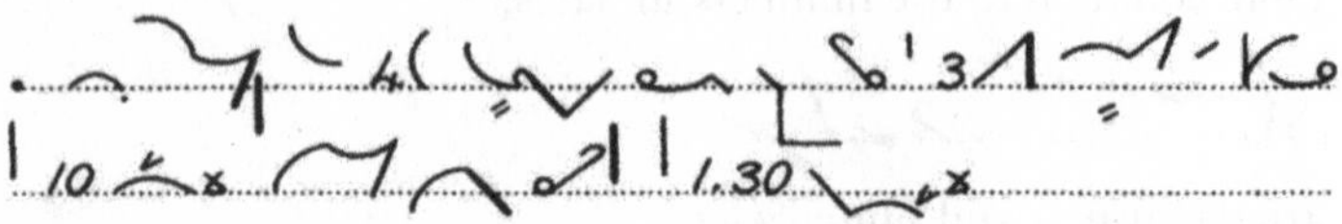 _[shorthand outline]_

(b)  _[shorthand outline]_

(c) 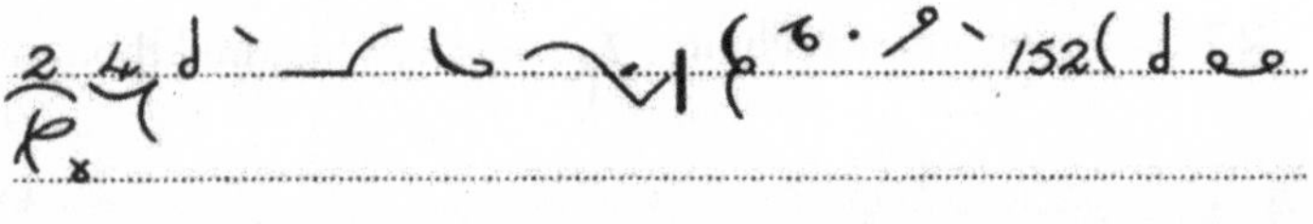 _[shorthand outline]_

(d) ....

(e) ....

Negative words

English uses several prefixes to mean no, not or opposite. The chief of these are IN-, UN-, and NON-.

IN- AND UN-

At the simplest, IN- or UN- may be shown with an N stroke and vowel, as in:

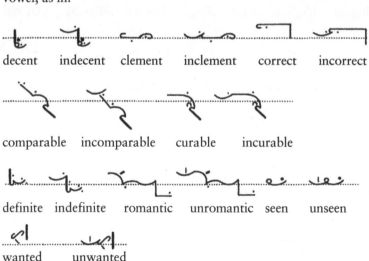

decent   indecent   clement   inclement   correct   incorrect

comparable   incomparable   curable   incurable

definite   indefinite   romantic   unromantic   seen   unseen

wanted   unwanted

The same rule applies even when the root word begins with N:

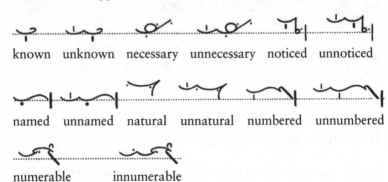

known unknown necessary unnecessary noticed unnoticed

named unnamed natural unnatural numbered unnumbered

numerable innumerable

When IN- is affixed to words beginning with L, M, R, it is coalesced into IL-, IM-, IR-, and the first consonants are repeated as shown:

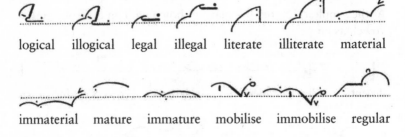

logical illogical legal illegal literate illiterate material

immaterial mature immature mobilise immobilise regular

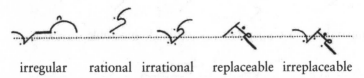

irregular rational irrational replaceable irreplaceable

NON-

The prefix NON- can sometimes be joined, but may have to be disjoined in some words:

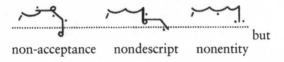

non-acceptance nondescript nonentity

but

non-essential   non-combatant   non-arrival

Suffix -SHIP

A stroke SH represents the ending -SHIP. It is joined when it can be joined easily, but otherwise it is disjoined.

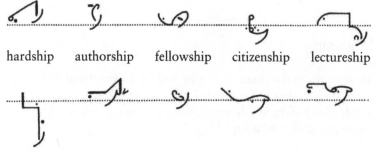

hardship   authorship   fellowship   citizenship   lectureship

dictatorship   guardianship   friendship   penmanship   craftsmanship

chairmanship

EXERCISE 62

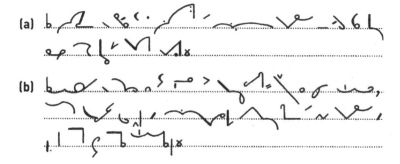

(a)

(b)

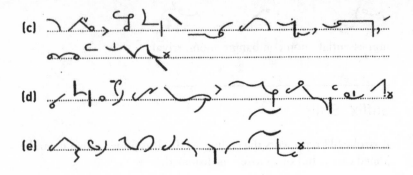

(c)

(d)

(e)

Disjoining

Most words in the language can be written in shorthand without a lift of the pen, but sometimes it is necessary to disjoin a part of a word. This is particularly so when there is no angle to show the joining of strokes of unequal length, as in:

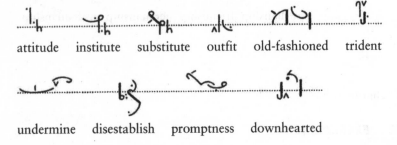

| attitude | institute | substitute | outfit | old-fashioned | trident |

| undermine | disestablish | promptness | downhearted |

Omission of a consonant

It has already been seen how a consonant may be omitted in order to make a phrase easy to write as in ⌣‾ *in fact*. When a P occurs between an M and a T, it is sometimes omitted in common words, as in:

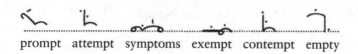

prompt   attempt   symptoms   exempt   contempt   empty

Vowel insertion

Once you have a good familiarity with the system of shorthand and a shorthand vocabulary of common words, most of the vowels can be omitted. However, it would be very misguided to try to do without vowels altogether. It takes experience to know when it is the right time and place to insert a vowel, but it is true that the more you can insert, the easier it is to read and transcribe your notes.

It is good practice to insert a vowel in these situations:

To distinguish common word collocations like .... *at last* from .... *at least*, or .... *in another case* from .... *in neither case*.

To show initial or final vowels where these are not indicated by a rule. For example, the initial vowel is not needed in .... *ask* or .... *art*, nor the final vowel in .... *penny* or .... *coffee* or .... *borrow*. In these, the rules indicate the vowels.

An initial or final vowel is very useful in words like .... *appeal* .... *element* .... *physically* .... *totally* .... *really*.

Diphthongs, triphones, and diphones are most helpful in quick reading and transcribing, and should be inserted as often as possible especially in short words, for example: ⌒ road

⌒ radio ⌐ doll ⌐ dial ⌐ cares ⌐ coerce.

In uncommon words it is helpful to include the vital vowel. For example, the word *egregious* will be uncommon, or even unknown, to many people. In such instances the key vowels help in ensuring that the word can be read: ⌐

Single strokes, and particularly single strokes without initial or final hooks or circles, and half-length single strokes, may often need a vowel if their reading is to be made easy. Words like *cut*, *lot*, *out*, *up*, *oppose*, *guide* and so on are better written with a vowel, and most experienced verbatim writers would do so, as in:

— cut ⌐ lot ⌐ out ⌐ up ⌐ oppose ⌐ guide

EXERCISE 63

(a)

(b)

(c)

(d)

(e)

(f)

Review

Read, copy, and then re-read from your own copy each of the three passages that follow. Then re-transcribe them back into shorthand from the key without reference to your original shorthand. Check the result.

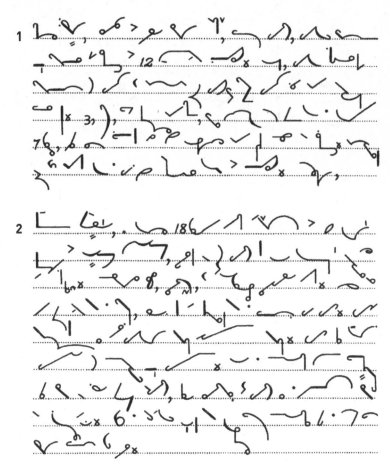

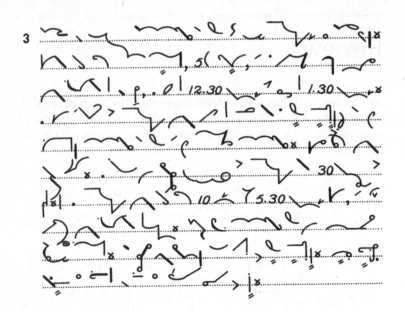

THINGS TO REMEMBER

▶ *There are shortcuts for round numbers, but otherwise numbers should be shown using normal figures.*

▶ *When a negative word begins IN- or UN-, the syllable is written with an N stroke and vowel.*

▶ *When the negative word begins ILL-, IMM- or IRR- this is shown by repeating the first stroke.*

▶ *The NON-prefix should be disjoined where necessary to produce a clear outline.*

▶ *The -SHIP suffix can be shown with an SH stroke.*

▶ *Vowels should be shown where it helps to make the meaning of an outline clearer.*

Keys to the exercises

Exercise 3

(a)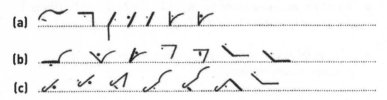

(b)

(c)

Exercise 4
(a) *We may make some losses on the day's sales at the Boat Dock.*
(b) *You ought to do the job of checking the boxes.*
(c) *You may go to the docks today to fetch the cases of soap.*
(d) *I ought to take the watches to the lads today as we said.*
(e) *I bought some of the locks and catches, but the lass at the depot said the boxes in which the things came had to go back.*
(f) *You may go in today and pay in the cheque to the bank.*
(g) *Nothing may change, but we ought to do something to aid the lads dwelling along the edge of the lake, in case it does.*
(h) *Some of us ought to fetch the spades and pails and take back the boxes in which the things came.*
(i) *It is too much to walk all the way and we ought to take the coach to the top; maybe we may pass you on the way.*
(j) *We may be at the game on Monday, and we ought to tell Jack and Anne because the two always come to the games at the Dell.*

Exercise 5
(a) *We may go to the bank today as it is on the way to the lodge and the coach passes it.*
(b) *I had some cases of soap and two bags of cabbages on the boat, but I suppose Tom had to take all the things in the boat to the docks.*

(c) *Some tell us we ought to locate the luggage at the coach depot and Tom knows the way to get to it.*

(d) *We aim to catch the coach at two which goes along the edge of the lake and passes the old gates of the lodge on the way.*

(e) *Tom has a tape of the jet coming in and all the things the lads said at the check-in.*

Exercise 6

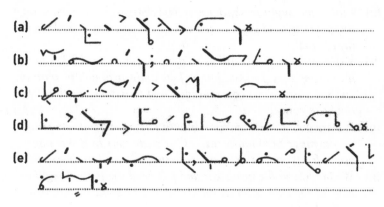

(a)

(b)

(c)

(d)

(e)

UNIT 2

Exercise 7

(a) *We ought to ask them to take the photos to the shop and thus save some cash.*

(b) *Follow the path along the vale to the lake and fetch them back on the boat.*

(c) *We may make a cassette of the songs they sang on the way to the cafe.*

(d) *You know the facts of the case and they show us the way to vote today.*

(e) *In the Gazette, Tom has an essay on the customs of the folk in the vale.*

Exercise 8

(a) *Thank you for the desks and chairs which came yesterday and which we despatched to our customers on the same day.*

(b) *Your message came as we were packing the rugs for carriage to the vessel Red Rose which will be in dock tomorrow, so we packed the dozen wraps you asked for in with them.*

(c) *We shall go to the bank tomorrow to pay in a cheque for the rail charges and for the repair work on the two cars.*

(d) *Have you mailed the customs form for the manufactures we are despatching to our customer in Rhodes? We referred to this in the message we passed on to you yesterday.*

(e) *I think we ought to share the repair charges for this work on the doorway and gates as we were both careless in parking the firm's cars.*

(f) *Will you be coming with us to the cafe tomorrow? I know that it is a long way for you, but as Jack and Carol will be with us and we are having eggs, sausages, and tomatoes, we think you ought to come.*

(g) *We are going to Rome for a month and taking with us some of our range of manufactures. Our customers in Rome have asked for them as they think they may sell well in the shops.*

(h) *We borrowed the firm's car and followed the path along the edge of the vale as far as the copse to take some colour snaps of the lake.*

(i) *We shall have to make repairs to the shed and in fact we have chosen Rob Wade for that job. We have asked Paul Shore to do the thatching for us.*

(j) *We think you are wrong in paying in so much cash to the bank today, as we shall have to have change for our customers at the sale of charms and badges in the shop.*

Exercise 9

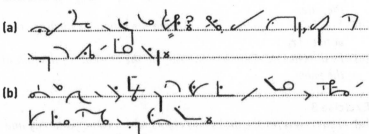

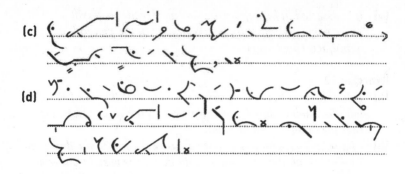

(c)

(d)

UNIT 3

Exercise 10
(a) I shall go to the college sports day and make some notes for the Sports Gazette, as they asked us to let them have something late in the day for the sports page.

(b) As I left our depot having worked all day I met our boss, a Scot named MacCabe, with spare parts for our car.

(c) In court, the judge said that the theft of some pots of jam was not such a small affair as was thought.

(d) We are manufacturers of coats and today we have sent two cases to the port for loading on the vessel 'Arab Rose' which will sail tomorrow. We were paid spot cash for the coats.

(e) I had a chat with the girls in the workshop, and they said they were waiting for soft soap to wash the walls of the workshop which have the dirt of long months on them.

Exercise 11
(a) We have to pay our rates tomorrow and that will affect our balance at the bank.

(b) We expect the results of our methods of manufacturing bolts and padlocks to show a rise though it maybe slow.

(c) Carol wrote a ballad which Tom reports will be on page 17 of the Gazette today, and I think we ought to mail a note to Carol on such a result.

(d) At the back of the catalogue are our estate cars and we show you the way to budget for the cars so as to save yourself a large sum.

(e) *It is asserted in his report that in this decade they will make some attempts to effect a change in the methods of manufacturing carpets.*

Exercise 12

(a) *I shall let you know tomorrow the date that the 'Gulf Rose' will dock which has as part of its cargo the cases of carpets that we bought a month ago.*

(b) *I have, in fact, sent a note with a customs form to the dock, and I would think that the cargo could be off the vessel tomorrow.*

(c) *You owe us two small sums for the manufactures that we let you have in March and May, but we expect you to deduct anything owing to you for the repair work on the estate car.*

(d) *Could you let us have tomorrow all the sports wear you have in the shop for us? Thank you for having kept them for us for so long. We are despatching a cheque for the sports wear today and you ought to get it tomorrow.*

(e) *I slept late, yet on awaking I felt doped. A cold bath had some effect and as I walked to work, thoughts came back and I recalled the tale that the tall Scot had told and resolved to take on the job of checking on all the facts.*

Exercise 13

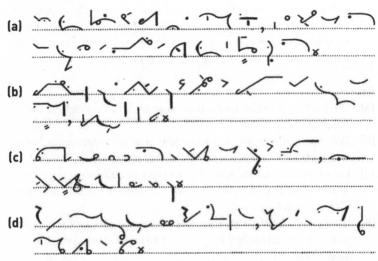

(a)

(b)

(c)

(d)

UNIT 4

Exercise 14

(a) *We have some places left at the Globe for the play on Wednesday but I expect we shall sell them tomorrow at the Club.*

(b) *Will you get a red and black table cloth and a dozen glasses for us? They are in the same place as the plates were.*

(c) *I am asking Tom and Carol to label all the customs forms. They may be young but they are capable of doing this job for us.*

(d) *Cut the cable in two with this blade and attach a plug to a length of it.*

(e) *We are going to classes in making clothes at the local college and we think this will enable us to save a lot.*

Exercise 15

(a) *I would be glad to know that the ropes and cables we despatched to you on the local bus have got to your depot undamaged.*

(b) *We think we shall be able to repair the gold plate and glass vases for you, but it may take us a month to do the job.*

(c) *Are you able to let us know who they are yet? We know nothing of them, nor do any of the local firms.*

(d) *We have two models of pedal car for the young and both of them are safe enough for babes.*

(e) *We are told by all those who know them that they are manufacturers of top class clothing, and that they may let us have the coats and jackets we are asking for.*

(f) *Put the tablets in this glass of orange and swallow them as you were told.*

(g) *We shall be going to Naples this month to talk to a firm that makes coach clocks, but we suspect they are not at all anxious to sell to us.*

(h) *They claim that the damage to the plates was the result of bad packing and the sample box they have sent back to us supports the claim.*

Exercise 16

(a)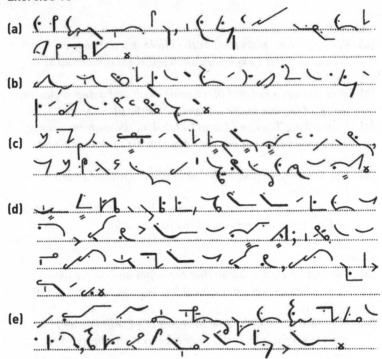

(b)

(c)

(d)

(e)

Review

1 *We have an unexpected balance at the bank and we shall be able to pay our work force a bonus on wages in a month or two. We shall also set apart enough to enable us to erect a depot close to the railway and the road. The airport is not far away, and we shall arrange to despatch some things that are low in weight in this way. It is our purpose to add to our estate cars, too. We shall call on all our local customers with the estate cars. In this way they will get the things they ask us for at low charges. We shall have to pay to make repairs and changes to all doors as a result of the law that will take effect in March, but two-thirds of this sum will be paid for us. The law says that local resources will be called on to aid firms in making such changes as the law calls for.*

2 *Tom and Edna Edwards settled in this vale with Rhondda not far away. They had Welsh forebears and in young days they stayed with Welsh aunts and uncles. So they came to Wales and they have stayed. They go to chapel on Sundays and work for the chapel clubs on Mondays and Wednesdays. Tom takes the lads for wrestling and sports. Edna takes charge of the netball club. This month the club is top of the local netball table and will go to Wrexham to play for the Welsh Netball Cup. Tom is an expert angler and goes off to the lake on Saturdays. It is rare for Tom not to have caught some perch or roach.*

3 *We were at the market all day yesterday and we bought a lot of things. The shops in the market-place all have planks on trestles with canvas tops set up in the road exposed to the air and the dirt. But the old chapel that closed some months ago is also part of the market today and things like cakes and sausage rolls that would be affected with dirt and air are kept and sold in the chapel. We purchased a table and a set of four chairs, and we also bought as a job lot a large box of plates, cups, saucers, and glasses. This was a gamble but our luck was in. Among the things in the box were a dozen cut-glass vases worth in themselves the total sum we paid. That was not all our luck. We also spotted and bought for a song a large up-to-date globe of the earth – the exact thing that the lads had asked us to get for them supposing that any such thing were available. As we were loading the car late in the day, a lad came along to tell us that we had located the exact spot in a game called 'Select your spot in the plot' for a large bottle of Scotch, so we left thinking that this was our day.*

4 *We are unable, I am sorry to say, to let you have an answer. We have located the references you told us of but the fact is that all the boxes in which the notes were kept were so much damaged in a blaze some months ago that not a word of them could be read, so the Board sold them as junk to a local firm. Yet you may be able to get the facts, because we know that photos on a small scale of all the notes are available. We think that they are lodged in the bank vaults of the*

Bank of Naples in York. We are glad to enclose a form that the Bank of Naples has sent us which you may mail back to them asking them for a report on the notes that you have to have. They will charge for this, but we think you may well not object to that.

UNIT 5

Exercise 17
(a) *The team will leave for a meal at six o'clock and we have booked places for them all.*
(b) *I think you ought to read this book as it tells of a part of the world that you know well and I feel you would be pleased with it.*
(c) *The finance necessary to erect this building is being raised in a month or two and the family will be purchasing shares in the firm that is doing the work.*
(d) *It is the policy of the family to use some of the money they make in the market on building and they are easily able to do this.*
(e) *We are asking each person who calls for money to purchase boots for the poor people in the Far East and we already have a good sum which we shall despatch to them soon.*

Exercise 18
(a) *Your business in Leeds will take you near the Selby Road and in that road Mrs Peel lives, I think it is at 428 Selby Road. We used to take care of Mrs Peel's business affairs so I would be pleased if you would call and see if she is well.*
(b) *She is a good cook and the curries and goulashes she makes are at the top of the class. But she has a limited range, and if she cooks for you for a week or two you soon come to those limits. Some dishes she will not attempt at all.*
(c) *The lads are saying that our team will lose on Saturday because Bill Blake will not be able to play owing to a chill and the paper in which it is published is the Daily Gazette.*
(d) *Food is our business and we are making a big attempt to raise our exports of meat puddings to Italy.*

Exercise 19

(a)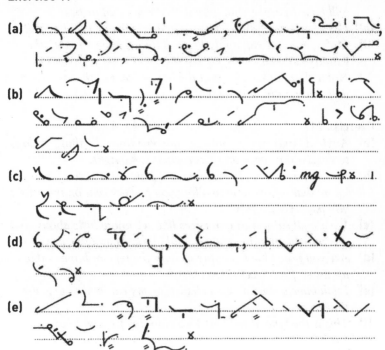

(b)

(c)

(d)

(e)

UNIT 6

Exercise 20

(a) *Do you think you could be at the tower in time to meet the boys who will have walked some miles by that time?*

(b) *This type of couch is right for your lounge and you ought to buy it.*

(c) *It ought to be light by the time we get up for our voyage on the lake.*

(d) *This invoice shows that we ought to have received eight dozen of these toys but we are four short.*

(e) *The red blouse suits you and you ought to buy it now along with that tunic that is lying on the couch.*

(f) *A long queue of people was waiting to get into the Avenue Market.*

(g) *It seems that a part of your revenue is taxed twice, and you will have to argue your case with the tax authorities.*

(h) *Have you some tobacco in your pouch? I would like a pipe, if so.*

(i) *Make sure that you apply in good time for the job with the County Council.*

(j) *Not a cloud in the sky, and the boys rejoice at this and they will enjoy a sail on the lake.*

Exercise 21

(a) *Anybody may make a mistake at some time; the thing to do is to check your work and put each mistake right.*

(b) *I refer to the invoices enclosed and I am pleased to let you know that we are able to allow you five per cent on the total if you pay by 24th July.*

(c) *We are all subject to influences that we know little about, and it is possible that the planets could be such an influence.*

(d) *Are you now able to supply us with the type of blouses that we asked for a week or two ago?*

(e) *I will have to buy a new exhaust for my car, and now is the time to do it.*

(f) *This is the type of tile that I was looking for and I have worked out that I shall have to purchase four dozen of them.*

(g) *The boys were loading the towels into the boot of the car at the same time as I was packing the boxes of toilet soap.*

(h) *The revenue raised by the sale of these piles of old tyre tubes and metal coils will aid us to fit out the Boys' Club.*

Exercise 22

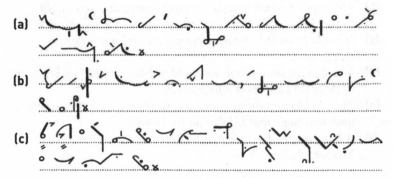

(a)

(b)

(c)

(d)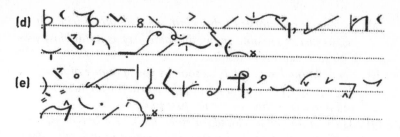

(e)

UNIT 7

Exercise 23
(a) *Let me have a note of the cost of these toasters and also inform me how many of them we have in stock.*

(b) *Some of the statistics that we ought to have for the study of our factory costs for the past year are still not available, and we ought to write about this state of affairs.*

(c) *Will you please assist us to move these stores into the next room as the next stage of the work is to install some oak chests in this room.*

(d) *I have had receipts for the cassettes you bought in Manchester and I still have just enough time to finish the books by tomorrow.*

(e) *A person who cuts vast blocks of stone into fantastic shapes is not necessarily artistic.*

Exercise 24
(a) *First of all we ought to stack all the cups, plates, and saucers in these tea chests and we should have the job finished by lunch time.*

(b) *We need to set a first-class standard of work because our work force in Chester will take this standard as a model for them to copy, and they made a thousand last year.*

(c) *If you have any spare time during the next week, I think you ought to study the Arabic alphabet and do your best to get it by rote.*

(d) *We think that James Stubbs will testify today that most of the waste stone that was to be loaded and despatched to the port was in fact sold to a local dealer for cash.*

(e) *As long as our stocks of china last, we shall go on selling it just as fast as possible and in the same way as we did last year with such successful results.*

(f) *Let us know immediately as soon as you spot any of this shoplifting gang in your part of the world for the first time and make sure that we are the first to know.*

(g) *As the store will be closed for stock-taking for two days, the repair jobs that need doing must be tackled in those two days and not left as they were last time.*

(h) *You will be able to get the stock forms that you need at the post office, but you had best get them today as they were almost out of them late yesterday.*

(i) *The largest stocks of steel rods of all sizes are at the Railway Works, so I suggest that we send a reliable chap to the works to select the best in the standard sizes we need for the job.*

(j) *It must be the best result for a month's trading that we have had for the past few years and most of it is due to the work put in by our sales force.*

Exercise 25

(a) *First of all, I would like to say that last year we assessed the value of the legacy at $8,000, but now it must be twice as valuable.*

(b) *In the local post office I saw a notice saying that the zoo might have to close because the area on which it is sited is to be sold to a large sawmill business.*

(c) *I should really like to have a report on this subject as soon as possible though I realise that the policy of the agency is to delay as long as possible in sending you all the facts. Ideally, I should like to have it sometime in the next week.*

(d) *It was easy for them to do the work set in the spare time they had at the end of each day's classes, but we had essays to write, so we had to work far into the night.*

(e) *We really think that they ought to co-operate with us in making a video called 'How to Type'. They have the right camera, and we have all the audio gear.*

Exercise 26

(a) *We hope you will be able to come to the New Homes Show. We usually have garage space available, and we shall be happy to keep a space for you in the car park and a room in the hotel if you let us know in time which day you will be coming.*

(b) *A new highway is to be built and some old houses and the rugby team's clubhouse will have to be bulldozed. They will all be unhappy about this, but new homes and a new clubhouse are to be erected nearby.*

(c) *It is hard to get rid of a bad habit. The thing to do is not to let such a habit develop. Yet it is possible by hard work and will power to shed the most deep-rooted habits.*

(d) *We now have eight vehicles and four warehouses and depots, two of which are leasehold and two of which we own.*

(e) *You ask me about Tom Hall. I met him first of all on a horse-riding course at Harrogate and I liked him immediately. As for Hannah Hall, I met her a year or two ago in the Black Horse Hotel and I was captivated by her charm and beauty.*

(f) *If he is still in New York, you should send him a message immediately, and I hope that it will be possible for him to visit Harry Hawke in the hospital, which is a few miles outside New York.*

(g) *I hope he will adhere to the scheme as we wrote it at the time and not attempt to change it in any way at all.*

(h) *We have a lawyer for all our legal business and he is the best person with whom to discuss the purchase of the two houses and of Hill Farm which, I hear, is in need of extensive repairs.*

Exercise 27

(a)

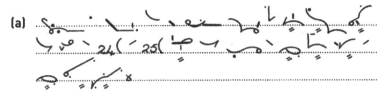

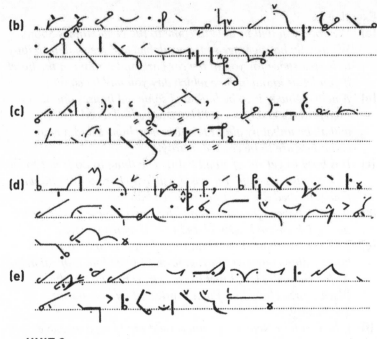

(b)

(c)

(d)

(e)

UNIT 8

Exercise 28

(a) *Our problem is that the price of these crops is too high for us to buy them just now, yet we shall be in trouble without them.*

(b) *The group now embraces several firms and shows an impressive growth, now that we have works managers of vigour and a labour force interested in producing to get bonus wages.*

(c) *We have increased the number of word-processors in those offices that have a great deal of repeats and duplicated work to do.*

(d) *We manufacture soft drinks and in October and November we faced serious problems because our water supplies were cut off for several days. At the same time, as the result of a transport dispute, we could get no sugar.*

(e) *As our sales have increased, we have had to take on labour in the registry to cope with the filing and the extra ledger entries. We need a new system.*

Exercise 29

(a) *At the hospital they said that he was in a state of stress, and they prescribed a holiday with his family in Cyprus.*

(b) *I was willing to accept that he could not get the screws in straight, but the last straw was his striking them in with a mallet.*

(c) *He subscribes to the view that it is better to segregate boys and girls at this stage though he admits you sacrifice a lot by so doing.*

(d) *I regret that we are unable to duplicate this fabric or replace present stocks.*

Exercise 30

(a) *This shop window display is interesting and attracts the notice of most passers-by. It gets its message across in a bright and direct way and has increased the sales of the products that are displayed.*

(b) *Dear Madam, We thank you for the interest you show in the gold bracelets we have on show. A leaflet is enclosed telling you all about these low-priced products. Yours truly*

(c) *The number of persons of school age is falling and so it was agreed at a meeting of the council that the number of teachers in the employ of the local authority should be reduced.*

(d) *Dear Sir, I am sorry that you have had trouble in getting your hedge-cutter to work properly. We think that this booklet will instruct you in the correct method of adjusting the cutter. Yours faithfully,*

(e) *I think that this branch has really worked hard at the problem of reducing the total volume of paper used and a decrease of 27 per cent for the period February to April inclusive illustrates this well.*

(f) *Please leave your address with the girl at the desk and we will send the parcel of Christmas crackers on to you as soon as it arrives here.*

(g) *The Wholemeal Loaf Company Limited sells first-class bread and so, according to the trade papers, business is growing larger month by month, in particular here in the south.*

(h) *The purpose of asking all these people here today was to get them to subscribe money to express support for our candidate,*

*Mr. Mark Strong, but the trouble was that we allowed too
great a liberty to our speakers who spoke for too long and lost
the interest of the crowds in the hall.*

Exercise 31

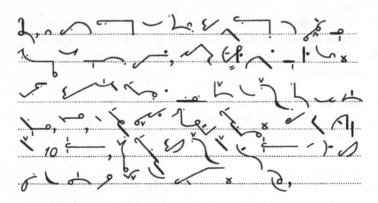

Review

1 *Dear Sirs, Thank you for your prompt reply to our*   10
   note about your paper supplies. We are sorry that the   20
   type of paper which we have supplied you with for   30
   so long is not available. The manufacturers tell us that   40
   the trade has ceased to ask for this particular paper   50
   because of its high cost. They do add though that   60
   they are still prepared to make this paper at the   70
   same price if you will take a gross of reams   80
   at a time. Will you please let us know if   90
   you agree to this. In the meantime we shall send   100
   you tomorrow a dozen reams of the type we suggested   110
   to replace the paper you always buy. We are sure   120
   that you will like it. Yours faithfully,   127

2 *Dear Mrs. Rogers, We are told by Mr. Peter Baker*   10
   that you are looking for a reputable firm of long   20
   standing in the trade to modernise your home in King's   30
   Cross. According to Mr. Baker, the principal task is to   40
   unite the present lounge and breakfast room into a larger   50

lounge, and also to build on to the rear of   60
the premises a large glass and cedar wood sun lounge   70
with a light-admitting hard plastic top. We have had   80
21 years of this type of work and, although   90
it may seem an exaggerated claim, we assure you that   100
we have always managed 10 satisfy all our customers. They   110
are happy with the excellence of the work and also   120
with the prices charged. May we call on you at   130
a time suitable to you, to discuss the subject? We   140
shall be glad to show you our leaflets and files,   150
and to let you have an estimate for the work   160
that you wish to have executed. Please call on   169
36013496 and ask   180
to speak to Mrs. Sue Blake. Yours sincerely,   188

3 *In the last two decades, the most popular way of*   10
taking a bath has become (if I may put it   20
this way) to take a shower. Showers are now installed   30
in 72 per cent of the country's bathrooms, and   40
in some English-speaking countries, the percentage is still   50
[higher.
Showers have become popular for several reasons.   60
[A thorough washing
process is much easier in a shower. Less water is   70
used. At the end of a bath you are lying   80
in – not to mince words – dirty water. In the shower   90
the water is always clear. A shower is invigorating, too.   100
You step out feeling a new person. A last merit   110
of the shower is that you may shampoo your hair   120
and scalp at the same time.   126

4 *Dear Miss Crow, Thank you for applying for the post*   10
of medical secretary to the Senior Registrar of this hospital   20
and for the detailed notes you sent us of your   30
successes in your college course and the report signed by   40
your Principal. We think it a most impressive record. We   50
hope you will be able to come for a short   60
two-minute test at a hundred words a minute at   70

two o'clock on Thursday, 15th September. The test will be   80
followed immediately by a talk with the Senior Registrar   90
                                                                [and
the Hospital Secretary. We shall pay for your fares and   100
your lunch. Will you please call me on the office   110
number at the head of this sheet to let me   120
know if you will be able to come. We look   130
forward to seeing you. Yours sincerely,   136

UNIT 9

Exercise 32

(a) It is known that this man will need a loan if he is to buy the two vans that he has to have for his work.

(b) He earns his money by dealing in old iron and he now has a fine business.

(c) The unions object to these new machines because, they say, the men who work them should get extra allowances.

(d) The judge was asked to assign marks up to a maximum of 10 based on the excellence of the taste of each sample of jam and to telephone the results of his marking to the paper.

(e) In Venice I had an illness and was rushed to hospital in an ambulance. They examined me and announced that I would be able to leave on the next day.

Exercise 33

(a) I hope to arrange a settlement of the debt owed by Mann and Sons and I shall use the trust fund for this purpose.

(b) I expect payment to be made for the plot of land soon, as I have reminded them that they still owe the money.

(c) The patient is now on the mend and we hope to arrange for her discharge if we get the Registrar's assent.

(d) His gallant act has added to the fame of the regiment and, I fancy, is sufficient to earn him an award.

(e) I lent my landlord a copy of the Land Act of 1980 in which a tenant's rights and duties are listed, but I fancy he found that document hard reading.

Exercise 34

(a) *We are particularly pleased that you will be able to make the arrangements for the main event to be put on not too late in the evening.*

(b) *I am arranging for your party to have an excellent lunch at the Fine Foods Cafe and then to be brought to the venue for the game by coach.*

(c) *It must be said that in the past year we have earned larger sums than in the last year of trading, and we have also paid back all our loans.*

(d) *The last time we met was in the post office because I recall that you had your van waiting outside and asked me if I would care for a lift to Union Lane to watch the big match.*

(e) *As a business man, you ought to take steps right away to raise the finance you will need for the purchase of heavy wire fences for which the local authority will make you an allowance.*

(f) *We are arranging for the new machines to be picked up by a heavy van some time tomorrow, and I will let you know by telephone immediately the van leaves.*

(g) *I had to pay a fine of two hundred dollars, one hundred on the spot and the balance within four days, and I also had to promise to keep silent about the money I had found.*

(h) *Dear Sir, Now is the best time to invest in the Alliance Investment Trust as the share market is rising and will rise, we think, for the next two months. We will arrange the sum you invest in any one of six ways, the details of which are shown in the enclosed booklet. Your money will be in safe keeping and we guarantee an interest rate of at least eight per cent for the year. In fact, we expect it to be much higher than that. Yours truly,*

Exercise 35

(a) *I think you can win this race if you run as fast as you did yesterday in training.*

(b) *To maintain all the machines that we use in this factory, it is necessary for our men to follow a regular routine, and they begin work as soon as the day shift have done work for the day.*

(c) *This region is largely urban and so we have a good bus and train service running into the main cities.*

(d) *All our residences are fitted with the most modern appliances and the response to our sales campaign has been most encouraging.*

Exercise 36

(a) *Spend the next few seconds counting up how many one pound coins you find in your till.*

(b) *It is important for us not to depend too much on any assistance we can get in painting the club house, but make plans for doing the whole job alone, possibly with nobody to lend a hand.*

(c) *I asked my assistant to look back at the correspondence we had with Tony Kent about the proposed training programme that we intended to run at that time.*

(d) *I want you to find out for us the extra distance we have to go if we decide to go round by the lake instead of using the main road.*

(e) *I think this is Dan's handwriting without any doubt, and so we have to accept that he took his chances and by some means made his way to the Lebanon and was in that country on 14th June.*

Exercise 37

(a) *The responsibility for the sales department is your own for the whole of next week, and the campaign that begins on selling cans of soup will be in your hands.*

(b) *Poach some eggs and open a tin of beans. I do not think that we have time for anything better than that if we are to reach the training camp by noon.*

(c) *We have been asked to return the screen of the VDU to the makers as soon as they can get one to us to replace the faulty one, so that we shall be able to carry on without a pause.*

(d) *I think this appliance is much better than the one we tested in June, and so it has been decided to return that one and buy four of these, even though the expense is greater than we expected.*

(e) *Please let us have at once full particulars of all residences you have for sale in this region, particularly those with large kitchens and well maintained.*

(f) *The ice dance programme is due to begin at seven o'clock and so we must arrange to adjourn our meeting at least an hour earlier than that to enable us to watch it.*

(g) *Go round the shops of the whole region and record the prices in each shop of all the paints in this list. They will not all stock the lot, but it is important for us to get our own list of prices and not to be dependent upon the lists handed on to us by the sales department.*

(h) *Our expenses this week are higher than they were last week, but that is because we have been going longer distances to get the kind of assistants that we need.*

Exercise 38

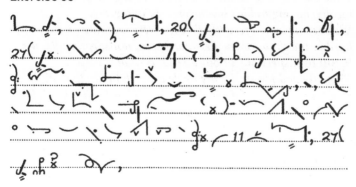

UNIT 10

Exercise 39

(a) *I shall not make any payment of my rates until I have a new assessment on my property.*

(b) *The only argument he has is based on a document which may well be a fake if an analysis is made of its paper and ink.*

(c) *The department has just issued an announcement that only four appointments to the top grade of clerk will be made this year.*

(d) *The assignment that we were told to work on was to carry out experiments on the sample to test how strongly it was made and if the results of the tests shown in the document were wrongly based.*

(e) *Unless you change your plugs annually or at least make adjustments to the gaps, your car will go no better.*

Exercise 40

(a) *This experimental stretch of road on the A1 has been instrumental in helping us to devise methods of surfacing roads cheaply.*

(b) *We need these supplies urgently and we are wholly and totally dependent on them for the maintenance of our departmental work.*

(c) *My son diligently studied the arts and skills of a monumental stone mason, and he has certainly made a great success of it locally, having trebled his business in two years.*

(d) *We became aware recently that we were working increasingly hard in the shop for smaller returns, so, not surprisingly, we began to suspect one of our assistants of dishonesty.*

(e) *Mentally and physically my uncle is much better than he was ten years ago and his change of job has been principally instrumental in bringing this about.*

Exercise 41

(a) *I was particularly pleased to meet Sir Peter at the party and he talked to me for a long time stressing again and again that if we would take on the job he would make the money available.*

(b) *Ladies and Gentlemen, I am glad to tell you that our annual analysis of costs and expenses shows that we have once again been able to reduce these, although by only two percent. The value of spending time on this assessment lies in increasing the efficiency of the firm. The argument is strongly against those who think that it is just a waste of time and money. In the four years that the experiment has been running, the analysis has been instrumental in saving us four times as much as the work has cost. It is a wholly viable project and rightly, in my view, it is to be extended to our offices too, with the* full agreement of our staff who stand to benefit by better and better ways of working.

(c) *Dear Sir, Thank you for writing to us. We have persistently pressed the argument that the only way for the firm to rescue itself now is for drastic cuts to be made in many departments and the immediate appointment of a new manager. It is no use mincing words. Bad management at the top has been the root cause of our problems, and as a result our market has been diminishing for a long time. Yours truly,*

Exercise 42

(a) *We have adequate supplies of all kinds of garden equipment to meet any requests you may make.*

(b) *Answer all these questions quickly as the time allowed for them is quite short.*

(c) *By the time he was only 20, he had acquired several languages and was well qualified as a teacher.*

(d) *The prices we quote do depend, as you will realise, not only on the quality of the goods that we stock, but also on the quantity that you require.*

(e) *What you will need when you get here is a square meal and somewhere to sleep while you are staying in the village.*

(f) *We are holding a day of aquatic sports to raise money for the victims of the earthquake, and we are requesting your support.*

Exercise 43

(a) *Year by year the pace of change quickens and our resources are inadequate to enable us to keep our equipment up to date. We shall require money quickly if we are to keep going.*

(b) *It would have been a better year altogether if we had not lost a large quantity of liquid oxygen and some machines only recently acquired.*

(c) *Thank you for your enquiry and for the acknowledgment of the safe receipt of the language books. We shall be enquiring in the United States for your requirements, but meanwhile we are despatching the books you urgently requested today.*

(d) *The question is: Where can we find cloth of the quality that we shall be requiring soon in the quantities that we will need?*

Squires Textiles said that they would be able to meet the firm's requirements but subsequently they were forced to acknowledge that the job was too large for them.

(e) We have to bear in mind that what we see as a sale is, in the customer's point of view, a purchase, and that we have to work together with our customers. If not, they will go elsewhere.

(f) She is a quiet child but a bright one, too. She is always wanting to know about things and asking such questions as: Where does the sun go at night? Why does a cat purr? Where does the Queen work? When did we learn how to speak? and What was I when I was not here?

Exercise 44

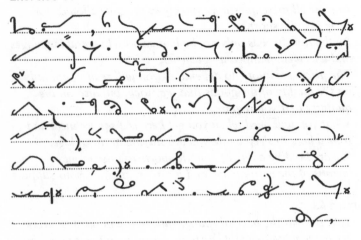

UNIT 11

Exercise 45

(a) I shall be free on Friday next and I hope to see you at the special general meeting of the athletic club when the new site for the hammer throw will be the subject to be discussed.

(b) I offered him two large crates of grapefruit at a favourable price, but he was afraid to accept them.

(c) During the war he rose to the rank of major in Royal Signals and he was flown to Vladivostok to attend the funeral of Marshal Donnell.

(d) *The energy for mining the minerals in this region was supplied by a powerful hydro-electric scheme which operates pile-drivers and steam-hammers.*

(e) *A new measure is being discussed in the House to increase the penalties on car owners who fail to license cars, either by heavy fines or by other penalties not yet decided upon.*

Exercise 46

(a) *I think it would be better for us to pass the summer in the civilised environment of this farm than to stay in a noisy holiday camp.*

(b) *We have a short filmstrip about the art and skill of nursery gardening and if you have a fertile soil and are ready to spend an average amount on advertising, then quite large sums may be made.*

(c) *Desert tribes are almost always noted for civility and for being hospitable and helpful to travellers. Life in those lonely wastes makes them all philosophers, like Omar Khayyam.*

(d) *I thank you for the privilege you grant me today to speak at this great meeting so that I may put the case of advertisement and of those who run advertising when so many are ready to criticise it on the grounds of its low morality or waste.*

(e) *Is this filmstrip about the Vale of York of any use to you? It is short lasting for only 30 minutes if the script is followed, but the photography in colour is really fine. I would sooner you had it than store it in the stockroom.*

(f) *Junior members of staff are presented with a staff manual on joining the firm, and they are required to read it and know what it says. The firm promises to care for the welfare of its staff especially its juniors and it fulfils this promise as the manual reveals.*

(g) *Numbers in the Civil Service have been steadily reduced over the past five years, but no dismissals have taken place; the numbers have fallen through change of job, retirement, marriage and death.*

(h) *Flights to all parts of Africa are quite frequent and they leave both Heathrow and Gatwick. Once a week they run a non-stop flight either to Cape Town or to Johannesburg during the summer months.*

(i) *An official of the Foreign Office was sent especially to meet these delegates and to be helpful in anyway that he could. The visit has the approval of all of us, and we hope that it will be beneficial to our economy.*

(j) *Free verse usually has no rhyme and no fixed rhythmic arrangement. This has led some persons to regard free verse as not verse at all, but in fact I hope today to show you some fine poetry, all of it written in free verse.*

Exercise 47

(a) *A large cache of ancient silver coins from Saxon times has been discovered in an Essex field near Saffron Walden.*

(b) *The government has decided to celebrate the anniversary of the opening of the river barrier with a festival to be attended by a gathering of all those who took part in its planning and building.*

(c) *The photographer, Stella Grover, is famous for her shots of clouds and weather and for buildings reflected in water. However, she may not win the Society's Gold Medal, which is likely to be awarded to her rival, Jennifer Gulliver.*

(d) *It is shameful that such a clever novelist should have been so little esteemed in her own day, and the discovery of an unpublished novel by her is a notable event.*

(e) *The government cavalry were manoeuvring to cut off the rebels who were engaged in the removal of art treasures from the old royal palace.*

Exercise 48

(a) *Miss Grover has done very satisfactory work for us in the enlargement of shots for commercial photography from normal size prints using the most modern types of enlarger, and she is certainly more skilled in this type of work than she was before she joined us.*

(b) *I am very glad that we now have someone influential on the Board to argue the case for better treatment for them and their customers.*

(c) *They arrived at the camp sooner than we had expected and more than a third of our party were not present to welcome them on their arrival.*

(d) *In our view, this new crop can be raised in all parts of the world and there is no doubt of its commercial possibilities.*

(e) *It appears that we may have gone too far in extending credit to these customers and so far we have only been able to collect about a third of the sums owed to us.*

(f) *In the course of his talk, the speaker said, that it is only possible to make an estimate of the manufacturing output of the new factories, and at the same time he warned those who owned shares in the group that it would be several months before we would have any more exact idea.*

(g) *Our customers have been very influential, dissuading us from taking any steps to cut down output for a month at least.*

(h) *In our own part of the country it is not possible to plant tomatoes outside until well into June and then there is less than four months to bring the fruit to ripeness.*

(i) *It appears that when they were about four miles along the road they decided that it was too far to walk all the way to their uncle's and so, of course, they called Tom, long-suffering as usual, who agreed to get the estate car out and pick them up.*

(j) *There is no doubt that there will be an acute shortage of green vegetables next month and it is only too likely that more will have to be imported from Europe and from Kenya.*

Exercise 49

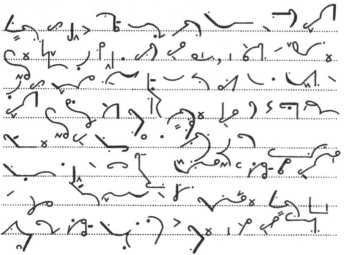

Review

1 *While every care is taken to ensure the security of*   10
these premises and of the car park, the management cannot   20
be responsible for any loss of or damage to customers'   30
property either in the hotel or in the car park.   40
Particularly valuable items should accordingly be handed   50
[in to the
clerk at the desk and receipts obtained. Our general security   60
measures work very well and we have an altogether   70
[satisfactory
record in this respect. The police carry out their annual   80
scrutiny of our security arrangements and the following   90
[is quoted
from the latest report: 'The Star Hotel has always   100
[implemented
measures that we have proposed to them and this has   110
been influential without a doubt in making them the safest   120
premises in our police region.'   125

2 *Dear Mrs. Nelson, It is possible that there maybe*   10
a delay of about a fortnight in meeting your requirements   20
of special inks and pens as some of these have   30
to be obtained in the United States of America. However,   40
we do not think that they will be any longer   50
than that in reaching you and you may rely upon   60
us to get them to you as soon as possible.   70
We have already posted the art paper you specified and   80
we are pleased to tell you that there is a   90
5 per cent drop in the price of this paper,   100
so we shall make an adjustment when we send you   110
the monthly statement. Yours sincerely,   115

3 *Dear Sir, You will not need to be told how*   10
hard it is to get approval from this local authority   20
for any building work that modifies or adds to an   30
original residence. One often has to wait for more than   40
six months even to get a reply to a request.   50
The Plans Department of the council takes a very much   60
harder line about such work than any of its neighbouring   70
councils. In your own case, we know that you have   80
been refused a permit to build on an architect-designed   90
sun lounge to your premises. We have formed a local   100
residents group with the support of several local councillors   110
                                 [to
change the policies and attitudes of the Plans Department.   120
                                 [Full
details of our scheme are enclosed and we hope that   130
along with many others in your area, you will join   140
us in efforts to amend the present state of affairs.   150
Yours truly,   152

4 *A country is no different from a family in the*   10
sense that it has an income from various sources, and   20
then has to budget how that money will be spent.   30
Like a family, a country can raise loans, but then   40
it has to take into account the interest that has   50
to be paid on those loans and also the repayment   60
arrangements that have to be made over a period of   70
months or years to return the capital borrowed. Where   80
                                 [things
differ lies in what happens when a family gets too far into   90
debt. Then the family will find itself faced by the   100
law and will be obliged to pay back all it   110
owes. A country may pay its debts by increasing the   120
supply of money. But if it does, disaster is likely   130
to follow. All prices of goods and services rise with   140
the most serious effects on employment and on all   150
                                 [commercial
interests. At the end of the day, the government of   160
any country has to be as financially accountable as a   170
family, if the people are to prosper.   177

Exercise 50

(a) *Vaccination against smallpox and inoculation against yellow fever are available on one day's notice at this health clinic.*

(b) *An extension of the time allowed for entry to this examination has been requested and the authorities will decide whether to grant this at a secret session on Friday.*

(c) *There is to be a national census of the population next year, and the public will be informed about it by means of a series of television programmes. They should attract a lot of attention.*

(d) *British people seem crazy about abbreviations and create a profusion of them, some of which endure like VAT and others of which quickly fade away.*

(e) *Inflation creates an illusion of prosperity, but it is false, and relations between various groups of the population are only made worse by inflation.*

(f) *It is not surprising that so beautiful and talented a woman should exert a great fascination on men and attract the admiration of both men and women. She is a highly successful professional lawyer and dresses fashionably at all times.*

Exercise 51

(a) *The oppression of some sections of the population is the cause of our present hesitation to go to the help of this government of so-called national socialists.*

(b) *I am glad that your persuasion was successful and that he agreed, though grudgingly, to the exclusion of these four illustrations because they would without doubt have been regarded as exceptionable by many.*

(c) *This new edition of the book with many emendations and additions will enable you to offer additional tuition to your classes.*

(d) *The job specification makes it clear that applications will be accepted only from those with 'A' level qualifications, even though it is only a vacation job.*

(e) *Your occasional co-operation in our operations to clear the cellars and basements of junk will be much appreciated, and* *will enable us to get on to the restoration of these vaults to their proper use once again.*

Exercise 52

(a) *Prompt attention to these provisional propositions for the acquisition of the Texas Oil Corporation ought to ensure our leading position when the final decisions are made.*

(b) *We are in a time of transition in our business when more people each week are realising the revolutionary sort of changes that are taking place in all office organisations.*

(c) *The notes you sent are unsatisfactory, and I want you to seek out much fuller information about all our living pensioners.*

(d) *We shall introduce some relaxation of our requisition procedures next month to cut down on the time wasted on waiting for decisions to be made before goods can be supplied.*

(e) *For your own protection, we strongly urge you to make reductions in your purchases and in your stock, and to take on the modification of all job specifications.*

(f) *I hope the sensational success of this new edition of your book will have given you satisfaction and that you will now go on vacation and accept the invitation to visit our tea plantations in Kenya.*

(g) *The word 'navvy' means a man trained in hard work, and it comes from 'navigators' – those men, often Irish, who came here two hundred years ago to build the inland navigation of the rivers and canals.*

(h) *Write an application to the Council for the erection of an additional hut on the site, and mark its exact location on the plans, attaching a specification of the hut.*

(i) *Ask the reception clerk whether it is far to the corporation offices as we have to put in an additional quotation by 4 o'clock for more supplies they need.*

(j) *Dear Sir, Thank you for sending us particulars of your educational qualifications and experience with the Bowman Paper Corporation. We are enclosing a copy of the job specification. The position is still open and we should like you to come to see us for a final selection meeting on Monday 15th April at 10 o'clock. All expenses will be paid. The selection*

meeting will end at 12.15 and we extend you a cordial
invitation to join us for lunch. Only one other candidate
has been selected. Yours truly,

Exercise 53
(a) I approve of the chief points in this report, but I wish the
survey had been made in more detail.
(b) The Salvation Army is very active in many fields of service
and deserves our full support in its work of tracing missing
relatives.
(c) The young musicians gave an attractive performance and
deserved the applause of the audience especially for their
sensitive playing of Brahms.
(d) At the cafe, they refused to serve us, and gave us no reason
why we were thought to deserve such treatment.
(e) Like the previous party held here, it was a festive occasion and
guests were active in seeking autographs from the stars who
were present.

Exercise 54
(a) I had no difficulty in getting their active approval to our
proposal to buy her some attractive gift to celebrate her
anniversary.
(b) We are out of stock of a number of the items that you
have asked us to reserve for you and in particular silk
handkerchiefs.
(c) Will you please reserve for me a copy of the new juvenile
magazine which will appear for the first time next week in
spite of difficulties over the printing. It will be called 'Young
Achievement'.
(d) One thing that we have learned in our survey of the traffic
passing through our chief city in the West is that we need to
provide more one-way facilities in the city.
(e) My wife has a number of male relatives who have served in the
armed forces and she knows very well how restrictive such a
life may be from a social point of view.
(f) I want you to observe this instrument closely. It is very
sensitive and it will register every change in the graphs you see

on the visual display unit once every five minutes. You will record the changes in pressure, heat level and flow of water as they flash up on the screen.

(g) *This aircraft will take off at 6.30 pm and the flight will last for ten hours giving each pilot five hours of duty, but they will share the time as agreed between them.*

(h) *He is a tough but attractive-looking man, talkative but always ready to listen and much more sensitive to any situation than he seems to be on the surface.*

(i) *We have a new range of fine kid gloves now available at all our branches and it would be to your advantage, if you have a little time to spare, to inspect them. These gloves, which have been bought as part of the stock of a warehouse damaged by fire, are of very high quality and are being sold at a low profit margin.*

Exercise 55

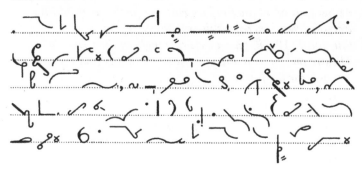

UNIT 13

Exercise 56

(a) *Thank you for your letter and for your order for two new electric motors for the stand-by lighting in your theatre.*

(b) *In the manufacture of clothes, natural materials have largely given way to alternatives like polyester and terylene which are man-made.*

(c) *I shall attend for another interview for this post at the International Trust Fund and I suppose I have a moderately good chance of success.*

(d) *Julius Caesar was really the inventor of our modern calendar and largely the builder of the Roman Empire, too, carving out the frontiers in the north and west of Europe.*

(e) *The arterial road is sure to be very crowded at Easter and neither of us wishes to stand for hours in long traffic tailbacks so I suggest we take another day's holiday and go by the alternative route on Thursday.*

Exercise 57

(a) *If you are a good operator on a typewriter, it is easy to become a good operator on the keyboard of a word processor.*

(b) *The printer tells us that he cannot get more than a quarter of the copies we need off to the distributor today.*

(c) *If you use the duplicator, then I expect to see your signature in the book which is inspected by the directors quarterly.*

(d) *At the end of this quarter our agriculture will be producing 62 per cent of all the food we eat, and further expenditure on tractors would increase this still more.*

(e) *Our local MP will give a lecture tonight in the Crucible Theatre on the structure of agriculture in this country and the outlook for the future.*

Exercise 58

(a) *I think there is good reason for his sister and his father to refuse to surrender to him their rights to his mother's effects.*

(b) *One of the most outstanding features of life in some country villages is the way in which the people are always ready to help one another in the event of a need arising.*

(c) *My dear Madam, In reply to your enquiry we can use an alternative material for tiling the floor of your kitchen, but it is much more expensive. We enclose another revised estimate. Yours truly,*

(d) *What a wonderful January we have had with the temperature not falling below freezing point on a single day, and no wintry weather at all, and a moderate amount of sunshine.*

(e) *If there is some other way of getting to this hill farm that avoids a long journey along the arterial road, especially when towing a tractor, I hope somebody will tell me.*

(f) The quarterly returns on all furniture, fixtures and fittings in this public house with the addition of any further items added since the last returns were made, are now due.

(g) The doctor told her to take 5ml of the mixture twice a day, and on the subject of food he said she must alter the whole nature of her diet.

(h) We have been there before and as a matter of fact the last time we were there, you may recall that neither of us could think of the name of the farm.

(i) It is only natural that, if we owe him this money and the debt is a long-standing one, he should send us a reminder. According to the calendar, he has been waiting for his money for eight weeks.

Exercise 59

(a) I hope this conference will be conducted in a way that will be congenial to all those attending.

(b) The company is facing some very complex conditions in the next few months and it is important that the new computer should be installed as quickly as possible.

(c) I am confident that the committee will give you constant support during the weeks of difficult work ahead, and that you will complete the task and come to a satisfactory conclusion of your mission.

(d) We must concentrate our whole attention on a satisfactory drafting of the terms of the contract because the Board is concerned that it may not be ready in time.

(e) In spite of all the TV advertising, you have to recognise that most aircraft seating is uncomfortable and cramped, and that better arrangements should be made, particularly on long hauls, to reduce this discomfort.

(f) It is incumbent on you to take the lead, and I recommend that you prepare a short speech in which it is recognised that our annual grant has been an encumbrance on the estate for too long.

Exercise 60

(a) We hope to bring the harvesting of the wheat to a successful conclusion notwithstanding the damp conditions.

(b) *You have paid too much income tax this year and I shall continue to press for the inland revenue officers to consent to an immediate rebate.*

(c) *Although modern technology enables a computer to communicate with another computer without the need for human intervention, nevertheless it remains true, contrary to what some people believe, that the computer requires human skill and brains to actuate it.*

(d) *I recommend that this line which has suffered a considerable fall in sales over the past year should be discontinued.*

(e) *In connection with the report by the Communications Committee published a week ago, we have received a number of comments which call attention to errors of language and also of contents, and these are a matter of serious concern.*

(f) *The radio commentator was constrained to make an unconditional withdrawal of off-the-cuff remarks that he made at the conclusion of yesterday's programme called 'Conquest of the Unconscious'.*

(g) *The book consists of a complete history of human communications not confined to language only, but giving considerable space to non-verbal communication, too.*

(h) *In order to complete the contract, the company sent out a convoy of heavy trucks loaded with all the rest of the supplies that the contractor had ordered and we were congratulated on a successful conclusion to a very difficult enterprise.*

UNIT 14

Exercise 61

(a) *The meeting arranged for 4th February is now to take place on 3rd March and it will commence at 10 am. Lunch will be served at 1.30 pm.*

(b) *Special care is needed when dealing with figures. It is easy to see a mistake in a word, but much more difficult to see a figure error.*

(c) *Two million, four hundred thousand tons of coal have been imported this month and that is a rise of one hundred and fifty-two thousand tons since last month.*

(d) *Nine hundred thousand persons are unemployed in this region.*

(e) *The aircraft will take off at 0400 hours and is due to arrive in Palma at 0600 hours.*

Exercise 62

(a) *It is illogical to suppose that an illiterate and immature person could open this door since the method depends on the ability to read.*

(b) *It is unnecessary to remind you that the cause of the burst water-pipe is still unknown, nor have we yet found out who immobilised the repair truck and how the person who did it got through the gates unnoticed.*

(c) *Your replies to the questions asked by counsel were indefinite, incorrect, and sometimes quite unbelievable.*

(d) *He admitted his authorship when the penmanship of the manifesto was compared with his own writing.*

(e) *We hope that the friendship and fellowship shown here today will long continue.*

Exercise 63

(a) *She has an old-fashioned attitude to fashion, and the outfits she wears remind one of the sixties.*

(b) *They are proposing to substitute art for metalwork at the evening institute.*

(c) *The crash of a Trident aircraft at Slough undermined BA's confidence in this type and they are all phased out today.*

(d) *If the attempt had been made to give prompt attention to the symptoms, this death could have been averted.*

(e) *Treat all his empty boasts with contempt. He is no more exempt from the duty on imported goods than we are.*

(f) *Please hang my coat up in the hall cloakroom and lay out my dress suit and my only good white shirt.*

Review

1 *Dear Miss Constable, As a result of the recent spell* 10
of dry, clear weather, we have been able to make 20
good progress on the construction of the twelve lock-up 30

garages. Indeed, we have advanced the programme so well 40
[that
I am now sure we shall complete the project well 50
ahead of our penalty clause date. Would you, therefore, 60
[according
to the terms of our contract, please let me have 70
your cheque for a further £7,000, which is 80
the sum agreed as the last instalment of our total 90
costs of construction. I am pleased to hear that you 100
already have a waiting list of tenants for all of 110
the garages. Yours truly, 114

2 *Dr. Johnson, the famous eighteenth-century writer and* 10
[compiler of
the first full dictionary of the English language, used to 20
say that the weather had no effect on people's minds 30
and attitudes. Experience suggests, however, that in this 40
[instance he
was not right. Most of us are cheered up by 50
a bright, sunny day and depressed by a gloomy wet 60
one. When the barometer is rising we feel better and 70
work better. When it is falling we are not so 80
capable of good work. In a country like Great Britain 90
which is subject to constant change of weather, it is 100
not surprising that the weather is a regular subject of 110
conversation and comment. This is a point often noted by 120
visitors from other countries which have a much more 130
[stable
climate than ours. 133

3 *I am glad to inform all members of staff that* 10
the new cafeteria is almost completed. It will be open 20
from Monday, 5th April, and a range of midday meals 30
will be available at two sittings, the first at 40
12.30 pm and the second at 1.30 pm. 50
The whole operation of the cafeteria will be run 60
at cost by a Staff Catering Committee consisting of three 70

elected members of staff and three management members. **80**

[Details of

this arrangement will be published shortly. The company **90**

[will subsidise

the finances of the cafeteria by thirty per cent of **100**

the total. The cafeteria will be open from 10 am **110**

until 5.30 pm daily, and light refreshments **120**

will be available at any time. I hope that every **130**

member of staff will make use of this new amenity. **140**

All suggestions should be submitted in writing to the Staff **150**

Catering Committee. Miss Christine Baker has agreed to **160**

[act as

honorary secretary to the Committee. **165**

Notes

Notes

Notes

Notes

Notes

Notes

Notes